Printed by CreateSpace
Copyright © 2010 Carmen Calderone
All rights reserved.
ISBN: 1-58898-887-2

To order more copies, visit the following site:
https://www.createspace.com/3152311

The Genealogy of American Organized Crime
The 20th Century
The First 100 Years

Carmen Calderone

2010

TABLE OF CONTENTS

	Pages
About The Author	xi
History	1
In Order of Rank	11
Individual Families	15
Events and Dates	19
New England Family	25
New York Gangs and Independent Groups	31
Murder Incorporated	43
Genovese Family NY	47
Lucchese Family NY	67
Gambino Family NY	73
Bananno Family NY	83
Colombo Family NY	89
New Jersey Family	95
Philadelphia Pa. Family	101
Pittston Pa. Family	109
Buffalo New York Family	113
Rochester New York Family	117
Pittsburgh Pa. Family	121
Cleveland Oh. Family	127
Detroit Mi. Family	133
Milwaukee Wi. Family	139
Minneapolis Mn. Independent Group	143
Chicago Il. Family	147
Springfield Il. Family	167
Kansas City Mo. Family	171
St. Louis Family	175
Tampa Bay Family	181
Miami Fl. An open city	185
New Orleans Family	189

	Pages
Dallas Tx. Family	195
Denver Co. Family	199
Las Vegas Nv. An open city	203
Los Angeles Ca. Family	209
San Jose Ca. Family	215
San Francisco Ca. Family	219
Canada Family	223
Sicily Families	227
Pizza Connection	235
Suicides	239

Special Thanks To

My Cousin Frankie G.

THE INDUCTION

The inductee gets his finger pricked with a pin, smears a little blood on a picture of a Saint. They then cut the picture of the Saint in a few pieces, putting the pieces in the hands of the inductee and burning it. Then the oath is recited by both the inductee and the made man performing the ceremony in Italian.

THE OATH

Noi gli uomini onorati di queta societa vivono dalla pistola e coltello e muoiono dalla pistol e coltello. Come il ritratto del santo che sta bruciando nelle mie mana la mia scottatura di amina puo per sempre in inferno se io mai dovessi andare contro alcun membro o regole de questo onoro societa.

WHICH MEANS

We the honored men of this society live by the gun and knife and die by the gun and knife. Like the picture of the saint that is burning in my hands may my soul burn in hell forever if I should ever go against any member or rules of this honored society.

I dedicate this book to my grandfather
>   **CARMELO CALDERONE**
>   Born In Casteltermini, Sicily, June 6, 1876
>   Married Carolina Ginex, 1904
>   Born August 1880   Died December 29, 1952
>   1st Trip to U.S.A. Alone, September 26, 1907-Age 31
>   Aboard The Sannio
>   Return to Casteltermini, Sicily
>   2nd Trip to U.S.A., May 24, 1912-Age 36
>   Aboard The San Giorgio
>   Returned To Sicily Due to the Death of Oldest Son
>   Paolino, Born 1905   Died 1912
>   3rd Trip to U.S.A., August 29, 1913-Age 37
>   Aboard The Barbarossa
>   Sent for wife Carolina, Age 34 and two children
>   Giuseppe, Born January 22, 1907-Age 7
>   Died August 5, 1967 (My Father)
>   Marianna, Born October 28, 1913- Age 9 Months
>   Died December 7, 1963

They arrived July 24, 1914 aboard The Prinzess Irene
Another daughter, Stella, Born September 28, 1915
In the U.S.A., Died April 11, 2003
Carmelo Died June 11, 1964

Carmen & Carmelo Calderone

ABOUT THE AUTHOR

About the Author

In the area of New Jersey where I grew up, organized crime had its presence in two separate families. The men of these families were always well dressed and treated people to various things. In other words, they had money to spare, whereas my father, who always worked hard for a living, never really seemed to have money to spare, although we were probably the average middle class of the 1940's. If you saw an older Italian person, well dressed, driving a fairly new car, with many people showing him extraordinary respect, someone would always say, "Well he's connected" and you knew what that meant.

I grew interested in this phenomenon. I would read in the newspapers about Frank Costello or Lucky Luciano and others. As a young, impressionable boy, my interest developed further.

There came a point in the 1950's when I started to realize that some of these men were getting arrested and going to jail for long terms. It didn't seem all that glamorous any more.

That's when I said to myself, "I better improve." So I went to junior college at night, while I worked during the day.

In 1956 I started to keep track of everything I heard and read. I started to pay more attention to the increase in members of organized crime who were frequently killing each other. It certainly wasn't what I wanted for my future.

This is one of the reasons why, when I could find the date of birth and the date of death, for a crime figure, I list it. Young men of today who may be considering an organized crime lifestyle should note the difference between the dates of birth and death listed here. They will find that a very high percentage of these men died young. Even when they weren't murdered they still died fairly young. It is no wonder with the pressure they must have been under, not only from various law enforcement agencies, but from other Organized Crime members as well.

In the 21st Century organized crime won't consist solely of Italians or Jews but mobs such as, from Japan (the "AKUZA"), from China (the "TRIADDS") and the Russian Mafia, who deal in nuclear weapons, among other things.

This book provides the names of the cities that organized together in 1931 and the chronological order in which their hierarchy reigned along with their predecessors and some independent groups.

The following are the alleged, reputed names that have been accused, considered, suspected and assumed, coming up in the media, TV, radio, books, magazines, newspapers, etc. over the last hundred years.

Prior to 1931, the names listed may be considered Black Handers and/or Mafiosi.

The word Associate can also be used as Soldier or Member.

The order in which these groups are listed is from Northeast, starting with New England, moving West to San Francisco, then out of the country to Montreal, Canada and Sicily.

HISTORY

HISTORY

The island of Sicily is located on the southern tip of Italy. Over the centuries, it has been a strategic area for wars. The Greeks were known to conquer the island in 500 B.C. There were two large Greek populated areas on the island; Agrigento on the south and Siracusa to the southeast. In 415 B.C. the Greek navy was defeated off the coast of Siracusa.

Sicily was also invaded by the Phoenicians, Carthaginian and the Romans. The Goths drove the Romans out of the island of Sicily around 440 A.D. The island became part of the Byzantine Empire around 535 A.D. Saracens from North Africa replaced the Byzantine rule in the 870's A.D. The Normans became rulers of the island in the 1000's. They joined Sicily with southern Italy up to Naples and called it the Kingdom of Two Sicilies.

In Sicily certain men do not call themselves Mafiosi. They think of themselves as "Uomini d'onore", "Men of Honor" and the organization "Societa d'onore," "Honored Society." When Joseph Valachi testified in 1963 at the Senator John McClellan Investigation Committee hearings, American television gave birth to the term "La Cosa Nostra" – "Our Thing". The press latched on to it and it mushroomed from there.

Supposedly, the Mafia originated in the 13th century with the rape by a French soldier of a Sicilian girl who was about to be married. Her mother ran through the streets of the town yelling repeatedly "Ma fia, Ma fia" which means "My daughter, my daughter." The townsmen rose up and started to slaughter

French soldiers who, at that time, occupied Sicily. Sicilian men were close mouthed about the secret organization that from then on would rob, kill, or do anything necessary to protect their families and loved ones no matter who was in power.

After the French departed, the Spanish ruled Sicily and the Mafia organization remained intact. Sicily was next ruled by the Savoy who gave it to the Austrians in exchange for the island of Sardinia in 1719.

In 1734 Spain conquered what was called The Kingdom of Two Sicilies. The Bourbon family ruled both Sicilies in 1806 when Napoleon took over and the French ruled again. In 1815 Ferdinand I ruled Sicily.

In 1860 Giuseppe Garibaldi landed in Marsala, Sicily and freed the island of Sicily from the rule of the Spanish. It became part of the newly united Italy.

Through all these centuries and various rules, the people of the island had to survive; thus the "Honored Society" developed. Its adherents stole and murdered members of the governing party no matter who was in power. They took on a cavalier Robin Hood image by helping some native Sicilians, but first they helped themselves, and their immediate families, until they acquired enough money to purchase their own land, having been influenced by previous generations of landowners. They had been conquered so often over the years, by so many different rulers, that their reasoning was, "If I own these acres of land, no matter who is in power I will always own these acres of land." They would put their family and friends to work on the farm and produce and sell whatever they raised and all would share in the profits. This was how they reasoned. However, just as they stole and hijacked from what they call the rich landowners at the time, once they became landowners themselves, they would have to protect their own group from outsiders. This is the origin of the different groups and families of the 18th and 19th centuries, with their vendettas, all due to thievery and the murders of their extended family members.

Most of the various groups became segregated due to the

geographic areas of their towns such as Palermo, Corleone, Castellammare Del Golfo, Villalba, Catania and others.

In the late 1880's Italians from Sicily started to leave home because of the lack of employment on the island. They were tired of the poverty, tired of being suppressed and living in the ghettos of their towns. They were aware that America was a developing nation that needed laborers, mechanics, tradesmen and workers of all sorts. Both single and married men, with no education, but with enormous ambition, wanting to have a better life for themselves and their families arrived in the USA with high hopes. Along with them came the criminals of Sicily as well. They knew that where there was a dense population, there would be a strong possibility of success for extortion and get-rich-quick schemes. The Honored Society members were not formally educated, although there were a few exceptions. They were ambitious men who wanted to get rich quick without working long, hard hours for their money. They preferred to risk going to prison or being killed to gain what they called "respect" through fear. It would take too long to acquire any wealth at all by just working at a legitimate job. Such was the old Sicilian tradition for members of the Honored Society. They had been suppressed and poor for centuries and now the opportunity to flourish in the new country presented itself.

Since Sicily has many seaports, the groups started in cities such as New York and New Orleans, where there were also seaports. In 1900 Vito Cascio-Ferro the Capo Di Tutti Capi of Sicily came to New York and New Orleans himself. Later he returned to Sicily.

By the early 20th century many of the Black Hand had traveled to various parts of the country. Following them were the organizers such as Santo Volpe who went to Pittston, PA and Santo Trafficante Sr. who went to Tampa Bay, FL. Little by little they penetrated over twenty major cities in the United States.

By the early 1920's men of the Honored Society, with the backing in Sicily from the town of Castellammare Del

Golfo, had grown all powerful in many cities: Gasper Milazzo of Detroit, Stefano Magaddino of Buffalo, Joseph Bonanno of Brooklyn, Joseph Aiello of Chicago, Joseph Profaci of Brooklyn, Joseph Magliocco of Brooklyn and Joseph Barbara of Pittston come to mind. Cleveland had also been penetrated.

Joseph Masseria, who was not from Castellammare Del Golfo, had been in total control of Manhattan since 1922. By 1927 he felt that he was being cheated out of Brooklyn funds and tribute that he also coveted.

In 1927 Salvatore Maranzano arrived from Castellammare Del Golfo and he quickly wanted to expand beyond Brooklyn, into Manhattan. From around the country money started to flow into the Maranzano group to support a fellow Castellammarese.

On April 15, 1928 Gasper Milazzo, a fellow Castellammarese was murdered in Detroit for his support of Maranzano. This started what has been referred to as the Castellammare War. It was really the Manhattan Masseria group against the Brooklyn Maranzano group. Others from around the country helped fund the group they sided with. By 1929 Al Capone, in Chicago, hated Joe Aiello so much that he helped fund Joe Masseria. At this point, Capone was also very friendly with Lucky Luciano who had just been recruited by Masseria to join his group along with Luciano's associates Frank Castello, Joe Adonis, Vito Genovese, Albert Anastasia, Frank Scalise, Willie Moretti and Carlo Gambino.

Little did Masseria know that Luciano and these other young men that he brought with him from his own smaller group had their own ideas for the future. For some time Maranzano had been trying to recruit Luciano and his group of young men to join his group, but with no success. Meanwhile, small gun battles had been occurring between the two groups with both losing men.

In late 1929 Maranzano had lured Luciano to a meeting with him to try to convince him to murder his boss, Masseria.

The meeting was at a shipping pier warehouse on Staten Island. An argument ensued and Luciano was hung by the wrists and slashed across the face and badly beaten. He finally agreed to murder Masseria. He was then driven to a Staten Island street corner and dumped off. Police finally came by and took him to a hospital; he survived. In the midst of all of this, the Great Depression had begun and Maranzano wanted to feed his men by expanding his rackets and territories.

By early 1930 Luciano heard from his good friend Tommy Lucchese who was a member of the Gaetano Reina group. Reina was tired of paying so much tribute to Masseria for being his ally. He was secretly contemplating a more over to Maranzano's group. Luciano grew afraid that if this were to happen, Maranzano would no longer need him as an inside man to assassinate Masseria. Maranzano would now have Reina and his men as the inside people to do the murder. Luciano would then be expendable.

In February 1930 Gaetano Reina was murdered and Joe Masseria appointed Giuseppe Pinzolo as his replacement as Capo of the Reina group. This put Luciano back in a key position, again needed by Maranzano to be the inside hit man for the murder of Masseria.

Unknown to Masseria was the fact that Gaetano Gagliano and Gaetano Lucchese had already secretly joined the Maranzano group. However this was not unknown to Luciano for it was part of the overall plan.

Pietro Morello had his own group of extortionists and murderers. He was a nephew of the original Morello group of Black Handers. He had been an avid killer who had merged with Masseria in 1922 as his group dwindled and Masseria's group increased. He had become Masseria's bodyguard and advisor. It was thought that in order to get to Masseria safely, one would have to murder Morello first. This was also a stall for Luciano to tell Maranzano to give him more time. So Morello had to go – which he did on August 15, 1930. This quieted Maranzano for a while.

In the meantime, Gagliano and Lucchese grew tired of paying Pinzolo tariff that was dictated by Masseria. So, with the aid of another member of their group, Dominic Petrilli, Pinzolo was murdered in September 1930.

In October 1930 Maranzano stopped receiving funds from Joe Aiello in Chicago because he had been murdered on Al Capone's orders.

In November 1930 two major gangsters on Masseria's side, Al Mineo and Stefano Ferrigno, were murdered in the Bronx.

By the beginning of 1931 the impatient Maranzano kept pushing Luciano to murder Masseria. Luciano made still another excuse. Masseria's bodyguard and underboss, Giuseppe Catania, was an obstacle and he would have to go first. Maranzano did not care because he was losing men, too. Even Joe Profaci and Joe Bonanno, who were major men in Maranzano's group, had been threatened and were running scared. So Maranzano okayed the Catania hit so Luciano could get to Masseria sooner.

On February 3, 1931 Joe Catania was murdered and now the path was clear for Luciano to murder Masseria. He had run out of excuses, and he knew that if he did not commit the murder soon, he would be the next to go.

He called a meeting of his top associates: Meyer Lansky, who was the head of an entire group of Jewish gangsters, Bugsy Siegel, Frank Costello, Joe Adonis, Tommy Lucchese, Frank Scalise, Albert Anastasia and Vito Genovese. The plans were hatched.

On April 15, 1931 Luciano and Masseria went to lunch at a Coney Island restaurant. While Luciano was in the men's room after lunch, four men walked in and shot Masseria to death, while a fifth man waited in the car out front. The Castellammare War was now officially over.

Salvatore Maranzano would now declare himself Capo di tutti Capi (Boss of Bosses.) He gave a banquet in his own honor in late April, inviting all the five families of New York and another one in May for the entire nation of families, declaring himself the top boss of everything.

Luciano still had not reached the end of his final plan. With Maranzano declaring himself Capo di tutti Capi, he was no better off than with Masseria. The final plan had consisted of the demise of Maranzano all along.

Luciano toured the country that summer of 1931 to seek the support of various families. He received support from the families of Cleveland, Pittsburgh, Tampa and Chicago.

On September 11, 1931 Maranzano took his final breath. Four Jewish killers assigned by Lansky posed as Income Tax agents. Lansky knew Maranzano would not recognize them. They took Maranzano into his private office, stabbed him repeatedly, slit his throat, and shot him. The final nail had been hammered into Luciano's plans.

Ironically, as the killers were leaving the building, they saw Vincent "Mad Dog" Coll, an independent killer who had been hired by Maranzano, on his way to Maranzano's office to pull a surprise murder on Luciano later that same day. He was informed of what had transpired, turned around and left.

There was a convention for Luciano in October 1931 in Chicago where he reorganized Maranzano's operation and eliminated the position of Capo di tutti Capi. He felt each city's Capo should run their organization any way they saw fit, without any other person telling them how to run their city. He introduced the idea of a seven-man commission, consisting of one member from each of the five families of New York, plus one from Buffalo and one from Chicago. Later, two more were added; one from Detroit and one from Philadelphia. He also introduced a position within each family called the Consigliere. To this day, America's National Organized Crime families are set up in this manner.

In the 1930's and 1940's organized crime flourished with little or no resistance from the police or the F.B.I. With the exception of Al Capone and Lucky Luciano being sent to prison, there were very few others in high-ranking position across the country that went to prison. The smart leaders of various Mafia families chose to keep a low profile.

In 1950 Senator Estes Kefuaver's investigating committee traveled the country and, via T.V., radio and newspapers, informed the public about Organized Crime. The public developed a major interest in the subject. Between 1952 and 1957 the pressure seemed to abate.

On November 24, 1957 in Apalachin, New York the home of Joseph Barbara, the Pittston, PA family boss was raided. This was the biggest raid to date on organized crime. Over sixty high ranking members from all over the country were arrested.

J. Edgar Hoover and the F.B.I. had no choice now, but to take an aggressive position against the Mafia. News of organized crime was in the newspapers daily. Later, the pressure seemed to slack off slowly until the appointment of Robert Kennedy in 1961 to Attorney General. Henceforth, the pressure was on J. Edgar Hoover and the F.B.I. full blast.

As we know, President John Kennedy was assassinated in November 1963. Robert Kennedy stayed on as Attorney General under President Lyndon Johnson until 1964 when he resigned.

The official investigations seemed to slack off again at that time. They continued to slack off until Hoover's death in 1972.

With a new Attorney General appointed after Hoover's death, the pressure was again on the F.B.I. to investigate organized crime, and is still on today.

IN ORDER OF RANK

In The Order of Rank:

BOSS
UNDERBOSS
CONSIGLIERE
ADVISOR
STATESMAN
CAPO (May be in charge of one or more crew leaders and may be a crew leader himself)
CREW LEADER (Soldier in charge of other soldiers)
SOLDIER (Made man. One who has gone through the acceptance of a ritual)
ASSOCIATE (A non made man)

BOSS
Head of the family.

UNDERBOSS

The underboss's role was to have various acts that the boss ordered carried out in the early 1900's. Today he may have several legal and illegal enterprises of his own and is considered the second in line to the throne of boss

In the early 1930's in N.Y. Lucky Luciano, the boss, was by far closer to Frank Costello, the Consigliere, and had more partnerships and deals with him than with his underboss Vito Genovese.

CONSIGLIERE

In October of 1931 at a Convention in honor of Charles Luciano, he officially declared a position of Consigliere for each family. It was to be a man of honor who all soldiers and members respected. He had the boss's listening ear and the patience for the lower soldiers with their complaints. This has been over dramatized in books and motion pictures. More often he was a partner to the boss in many dealings.

Earlier in the twentieth century like in the case of Stephano La Torre who arrived in the U.S. earlier than the first boss of Pittston, PA, Santo Volpe, he became a partner in many of the illegal enterprises because he knew the area and the men of that coal mining town longer, therefore advising him of situations unfamiliar to Volpe. This became known as the Consigliere.

In Boston at the merge with Providence, RI with Fillipo Bruccolo as boss and Giuseppe Lombardo retiring as boss of Boston stayed on as Consigliere of the now newly formed New England family. The Consigliere was usually a partner to the boss in the old days but today as roles have changed it simply means the third man in line to the throne of boss.

ADVISOR

One who is brought in by the Boss to give advice on a certain situation, a so called expert in a particular field.

STATESMAN

A former member of high standing, now retired, also could be a former Boss brought in for their opinion on certain occasions of discussions.

BLACK HANDER

Extortionists and murderers in the early days, both in Sicily and in the U.S.A. such as the New York Morello Family.

INDIVIDUAL FAMILIES

In 1928 there were 22 groups across the United States

5 New York City groups	Buffalo, NY	St. Louis, MO
Boston, MA	Pittsburgh, PA	Denver, CO
Providence, RI	Detroit, MI	New Orleans, LA
Pittston, PA	Cleveland, OH	Tampa Bay, FL
Newark, NJ	Milwaukee, WI	Kansas City, MO
Philadelphia, PA	Chicago, IL	Dallas, TX

In 1937 Newark, NJ dropped out.

In 1938 Elizabeth, NJ joined in.

In 1937 Los Angeles, San Jose, and San Francisco, CA joined in, the total now, 25 groups, now called families.

In early 1940's Springfield, IL joins in.

In 1947 Boston, MA and Providence, RI merged into one family.

In 1964 Dallas, TX disbands and is taken over by New Orleans.

In the 1960's Rochester, NY breaks away from Buffalo, NY and becomes a separate family; the total is 25 families again.

In the 1980's San Francisco and San Jose, CA merge into one family, the total is now 24 families.

EVENTS AND DATES

The Genealogy of American Organized Crime   [21]

EVENTS

Turning points in the USA and Crime Conventions

Pre 1830	English arrive in USA in large numbers
1830-1880	Irish arrive in USA in large numbers
1881—1915	Jewish arrive in USA in large numbers
1888—1940	Italians arrive in USA in large numbers
1891	Lynching of Italians in New Orleans, LA
1890—1905	Newspaper circulation wars
1910	Mann Act passed
1910	Lupo The Wolf goes to prison
1911	Grand Master Enrico Alfano of the Brooklyn Camorra goes to prison.
April 6, 1917 to Nov. 11, 1918	World War I
1917	Pelligrino Morano of the Camorra goes to prison. Camorra starts to disband.
1919	Volstead Act
Jan. 16, 1920 to Dec. 1933	Prohibition
1921	Gasper Milazzo goes to Detroit, MI
1921	Stefano Magaddino goes to Buffalo, NY
1922	Masseria takes over Manhattan
1925	Johnny Torrio retires in Chicago
1926	Cleveland Syndicate formed
1928	Brooklyn Nicholo Schirio steps down for Maranzano
1928	April 15th, Gasper Milazzo's murder in Detroit

	starts Castellammare War
1928	Group Seven formed by Luciano and others
1928	Joe Profaci starts his own family in Brooklyn
1928	December 5th, Cleveland Syndicate Convention
1929	February 14th, St. Valentine's Day Massacre in Chicago
1929	May 13th-16th, Atlantic City, NJ National Crime Convention
	No families from Castellammare Del Golfo were invited
1929	October 24th, Stock Market crashed and Depression begins
1931	Purple Gang in Detroit, MI disbands
1931	April 15th, Masseria murdered, Castellammare war ends
1931	May, Convention in Wappingers Falls, NY for Salvatore Maranzano
1931	September 11th, Maranzano murdered
1931	October, Convention at Congress Hotel in Chicago for Luciano, Start of the new National Syndicate or the "La Cosa Nostra", Start of the Commission
1931	November, Franconia Hotel, NY Lansky unites Jewish gangs across the country
1933	December, Prohibition ends
1934	April, Waldorf Astoria, NY Convention for National Crime Syndicate, Italians and Jews merge
1934	Murder Incorporated formed
1934	Lansky goes to Cuba for first time
1934	Costello starts slot machines in New Orleans, LA
1935	September 10th, Governor Huey Long in Louisiana murdered
1937	Bugsy Siegel goes to Los Angeles, CA
1937	Los Angeles recognized by National Syndicate

1937	Newark, NJ D'Amico Family disbands
1938	Kansas City, MO Tom Pendergast dies
1941	Lansky meets with Batista in Cuba brings along his attorney, Richard Nixon
1941	Philadelphia Family moves into Atlantic City
1941	World War II begins
1945	World War II ends
1946	Convention in Cuba, Deported Luciano is in attendance and Frank Sinatra is the entertainment
1946	December 26th, Siegel opens Flamingo Casino in Las Vegas
1947	Providence, RI and Boston, MA join as one New England Family
1950	Kefauver Committee starts traveling the country
1951	March 13th, Senator Kefauver puts Costello's hands on T.V.
1957	May 2nd, Costello shot in the head, wounded and retires
1957	November 24th, Apalachin NY Convention raided by police
1959	November 8th Worcester, MA crime meeting
1963	September & October, Senator John McClellan investigation sub-committee puts Joseph Valachi on T.V.
1964	Dallas, TX family disbands
1964	Joe Bonnano steps down, retires to Arizona
1969	Rochester, NY splits from Buffalo family
1970	February 15th, Acapulco, Mexico Crime Convention discussion of gambling in Atlantic City, NJ
1971	June 28th, Joe Colombo wounded and Italian American Civil Rights League disbanded
1982	Entire Cleveland Family hierarchy imprisoned
1987	Four out of five NY bosses imprisoned

1992	April, John Gotti 5th , NY Family boss imprisoned
1996	March 14th , entire Detroit Family hierarchy arrested
1999	Detroit Family hierarchy imprisoned

NEW ENGLAND FAMILY

NEW ENGLAND FAMILY

BOSTON, MASS.-   Irish Gustin Gang, Late 1800's
Frank Wallace, Murdered 1931
Barney Walsh, Murdered 1931
Timothy Coffey

In the early 1900's the following were the heads of small Massachusetts families:

Lawrence, Mass.-	Giuseppe "Peppino" Modica
Springfield, Mass.-	Salvatore Cufari
Worcester, Mass.-	Carlo Mastrototaro
Arlington, Mass.-	Nazzarine "Nene" Turrussa
	Giuseppe "Joe Burns" Anselmo
Glouster, Mass.-	Giuseppe Palombo
South Boston-	Antonio Santonello, Died 1952
Boston-	Fillipo Bruccola, Born 1886
North & West Boston-	Giuseppe Lombardo
	Born: 1895
	Reign Peaked around 1925
	Retired
	Died: 1969
	Organized all the small Mass. towns together to become the overall Boss
Top Associate-	Charles "King" Soloman
	Career Peaked: 1928
	Murdered: January 24, 1933

Capo's-	Mario Ingraddia, Biagio DiGiacomo
Underboss-	Mike "The Wise Guy" Rocco
Consigliere-	Gaspar Massina, Joseph Russo

Other Associates of Lombardo were:
  Joseph Linsey, Reign: 1920's—1940's
  Joseph Kennedy, Hyman Abrams,
  Lou Fox (Revere, Mass.) Reign: 1947—1962
  Died: 1963
  Phil Gallo

PROVIDENCE RHODE ISLAND FAMILY

Boss-	Frank "Butsey" Morelli
	Reign: 1917—1932
	Stepped down for Fillipo Bruccola
	Retired: 1947
	5 Brothers
Underboss-	Frank Zagarino
Top Asso.-	Daniel Walsh
Boss-	Fillipo Bruccola
	Born: 1886
	Arrives from Palermo, Sicily in 1920
	Reign: 1932—1951
	Merges the Boston and Providence Families into 1 family in 1947 referred to from now on as The New England Family with him as "Top Boss"
	Retired to Sicily 1954
	Died: 1987
Underboss-	Henry Tameleo
	Born: 1901
	Died in prison August 1985
Cosigliere-	Giuseppe Lombardo

NEW ENGLAND FAMILY

Boss-	Raymond Loredo S. Patriarca
	Born: 1908
	Reign: 1951—1984
	Imprisoned: 1969
	Released: 1975
	Died: 1984
Underboss In	
Providence, R.I.-	Henry Tameleo
Underbosses In	
Boston, Mass.-	Carlo Mastrototaro
	Gennaro "Jerry" Angiulo
	Born: 1919
	Imprisoned: 1986
5 Brothers:	Nicholas, Born:1916, Died: 1987
	Frank, Born: 1920, Imprisoned
	Donato "Danny", Born: 1923, Imprisoned
	Antonio, Born 1925
	Mike, Born 1927 Imprisoned
Underboss to	
Angiulo-	Ilario Zannino
	Alias Larry Baiona
	Born: 1920
	Imprisoned: 1972, Released
	Imprisoned again in 1987
Underboss-	Peter Limone
	Sentenced to execution in 1968 and released
	Sentenced again in 1986 to 12 years
Consigliere-	Early years-Giuseppe Lombardo
Consigliere-	Frank Cucchiara
Boss-	Raymond J. C. Patriarca, Jr.
	Born: 1948
	Reign: 1984—1992
	Imprisoned December 1991

Underboss-   William Phillip Grasso (Murdered)
Consigliere-   Joseph Russo
Underboss In
Boston, Mass.-   Nicholas Bianca
                   Around 1990's
                   Died in prison 1994

Underboss In
Providence, R.I.-William "Billy" DiSanto
                   Around 1990's

Boss-   Francis "Cadillac Frank" Salemme
                   Reign: 1992 -1995 Imprisoned
Underboss-   Stephen "The Rifleman" Flemmi
                   Imprisoned Mid 1990's (Informant)
Associate-   James "Whitey" Bulger born 1929
                   (Fugitive)

Boss-   Louis Manocchio
                   Reign: 1996—?

NEW YORK GANGS AND INDEPENDENT GROUPS

Gangs in New York & Some Members

Forty Thieves-	started around 1825
Whyos-	Timothy "Big Tim" Sullivan, 1899, his protege, Arnold Rothstein and Herman "Beansy" Rosenthal Murdered 1912
Five Pointers-	Paolo Vaccarelli, Alias "Paul Kelly", 1905, James "Biff" Ellison, Johnny Torrio, Jack Sirocco, Charles Luciano, Al Capone
Plug Uglies-	Irish
Dead Rabbits-	Irish
The White Hand Gang-	Irish Early 1900's—1928 Dennis Meehan
Shirt Tails-	
The Westies-	Hells Kitchen, NY Mid 20th Century
Gophers-	Owney Madden, 1910
Bergen Ave. Mob-	Dutch Schultz
Broadway Mob-	Joe Adonis, 1918
Bugs & Meyers Mob-	Benjamin Siegel and Meyers Lansky, 1914
Bowery Gang-	Monk Eastman
104 Street Gang-	Frank Costello, 1912
Essex Market Courthouse Gang	Max Hochstim, Solomon "Silver Dollar Smith" Goldschmidt and Martin Engel, 1880's—1890's

Manhattan Lower Eastside Jewish Gangs at the Turn of the 20th Century

EASTMAN'S JEWISH BOWERY GANG

Boss-   Monk Eastman – born 1870's
Real Name: Edward Osterman
Reign: 1890's—1904
Imprisoned: 1904—1912
Murdered: December 26, 1920
Great battles with Paul Kelly
"Vaccarelli"
of the Five Pointers Gang in 1903

Boss-   Max "Kid Twist" Zweiback
Reign: 1904—1908
Murdered: May 1908

Boss-   Big Jack Zelig
Real Name: William Alberts
Born: 1882
Reign: 1908—1912
Murdered: October 1912
Gang members imprisoned earlier in 1912
Harry "Gyp of Blood" Horowitz, Jacob "White Lewis" Seidenschnier, Louis "Lefty Louis" Rosenberg, Jewish Black Hander, Joseph "Yoski Nigger" Toblinsky,
Pre 1913 Imprisoned: 1913

BOWERY GANG, GARMENT DISTRICT

Boss-   Benjamin "Dopey Benny" Fein
Born: 1889
Reign: 1912—1915 imprisoned
Associates: Joseph "Joe the Greaser"

Rosenzweig, Waxey Gordon,
Herman "Little Hymie" Bernstein
and Jacob "Tough Jake" Heiseman.

FIVE POINTER GANG
Italians & A Few Jews
Lower Eastside Garment District

Boss-   Paul Kelly
Real Name: Paolo Vaccarelli
Born: 1876, Sicily
Died: April 3, 1936
Reign: 1890's -1915
Joins D'Aquilla & Yale Gang in 1915
Vice President of International
Longshoremen's Assoc.
Other members of Five Pointer Gang
were Johnny Torrio,
Frankie Yale, Lucky Luciano and Al
Capone

Boss-   Giacomo "Jack" Sirocco (Later joins
Vaccarelli on the Brooklyn waterfront).

Boss-   Nathan "Kid Dropper" Kaplan
(Partner to Jack Sirocco)
Born: 1891
Reign: 1915—1923
Murdered: August 1923
He had 6 brothers.
Foe of Kid Dropper, Johnny Spanish
murdered July 29, 1919.

BOWERY GANG OF LOWER EASTSIDE GARMENT DISTRICT

Boss- Jacob "Little Augie" Orgen
A protege of The Old Benny Fein Gang
Born: 1894
Reign: 1923—1927
Murdered: October 1927
Bodyguard—Legs Diamond
Members of the gang: Louis "Lepke" Buchalter, Jake Shapiro

Boss- Louis "Lepke" Buchalter
Born: 1897
Reign: 1927—1939
Imprisoned: August 24, 1939
Executed: April 4, 1944
Joins Lansky and Luciano gang in 1929

Associate: Jacob "Gurrah" Shapiro
Born: 1899
Went to prison 1938
Died in prison 1947
A foe group of Lepke in Brooklyn were the Ambergs, Joseph, Oscar, Hyman "Hymie the Rat", and Louis "Pretty" Amberg, also the Shapiro brothers Meyers, Irving and Willie were all murdered by 1935 (no relation to Jake Shapiro).

The Luciano family and the Anastasia crew of the Mangano family pick up this district by 1940.

INDEPENDENTS NEW YORK

INDEPENDENT, INVESTOR, GAMBLER and TEACHER OF CRIME and RACKETS
Arnold "The Brain" Rothstein

Students:	J. Torrio, P. Kastel, F. Costello, C. Luciano, M. Lansky, F. Erickson, O. Madden, M. Eastman, L. Diamond, D. Schultz, W. Gordon, L. Buchalter, J. Shapiro & A. Zwillman
Born:	1882
	Partner on several ventures with Dandy Phil Kastel
	Dealings with Tammany leaders Charles Murphy and Big Tim Sullivan
Prominent:	from 1915—1928
Murdered:	November 4, 1928
	Older brother Harry Rothstein

NEW YORK INDEPENDENT in HELL'S KITCHEN

Owney Victor "The Killer" Madden

Carmen Calderone

Born:	1892, Liverpool, England
	Arrives in New York 1903
	Boss of the Gophers Gang 1910
	Shot 5 times on November 6, 1912 and survived
	Imprisoned for murder 1915, Released 1923
	Friendly with Luciano Gang, Gordon Gang & Zwillman Gang
	Retired in New York in 1932
	Went to Hot Springs, Ark. in 1933
	Made it a safeway town for other criminals
Died:	April 24, 1965
Associate:	George Jean "Big Frenchie" DeMange-died
Driver:	George Raft Born: 1895

NEW YORK INDEPENDENT GROUP

Waxey Gordon

Real Name:	Irving Wexler
Born:	1888
Prominent:	1921—1934
	Joins in Bootlegging in 1921 with Arnold Rothstein and Big Maxey Greenberg from Detroit
	Later Rothstein and Greenberg drop out of partnership
	By 1926 moves operation to Hudson County, N.J.
	Later deals with Zwillman
	Opens up distillery in Phila., deals with Boo Boo Hoff
	Feuds with Lansky
	Feuds with Dutch Schultz

	Imprisoned 1934—1940
	Sent to Alcatraz January 1952
Died:	in prison June 24, 1952
Associates:	Max Hassell Alias Gassell and Max "Big Maxey" Greenberg, both murdered April 12, 1933
	Fabrizzo Brothers - Tony, Andy, & Louis – all murdered 1932

NEW YORK INDEPENDENT GROUP – BRONX & HARLEM

	Dutch Schultz
Real Name:	Arthur Flegenheimer
	Bootlegging and numbers
Born:	1902
Reign:	1923—1935
Murdered:	October 23, 1935
Associates:	Abraham "Bo" Weinberg, Murdered September 1934
	Otto Biederman Alias Abbaddaba Berman, Born: 1880
	Murdered: October 23, 1935
	Barnard "Lulu" Rosenkrantz, Murdered: October 23, 1935
	Abe Landay, Murdered: October 23, 1935
	Martin Krompier, Frank Reither Alias Red Reed, Soloman "Solly" Girsch and Morris Schmertzler Alias Max Courtney

NEW YORK

INDEPENDENT, BOOTLEGGER, BODYGUARD, HI JACKER, HITMAN and DOUBLE CROSSER

Jack "Legs" Diamond

Real Name:	John T. Noland
Born:	1896
Prominent:	1922—1931
	Worked for Little Augie Orgen as Bodyguard
	Worked for Arnold Rothstein as Bodyguard
	Had over a half dozen separate attempts on his life, survived them all but one
	Was hated by all gang bosses in Manhattan
Murdered:	December 1931
	Brother Edward "Eddie" Diamond, Died of illness 1928
Associates:	Charles Entratta and John Scaccio

NEW YORK

INDEPENDENT, BOOTLEGGER, HENCHMAN, RACKETEER,

HITMAN, KIDNAPPER and HI JACKER

Vincent "Mad Dog" Coll

Born:	1909
	Worked for Dutch Schultz
	Feuded with Schultz and many other gang bosses
	On September 11, 1931 was deterred from murdering Luciano for Maranzano on the same day that Maranzano was murdered.
Murdered:	February 9, 1932
	Older brother Peter Coll, Born: 1907, Murdered: May 30, 1931
Associates:	Fiorio Basile, Patsy DelGreco

BUGS & MEYER GANG

Formed 1914

Meyer Lansky; Real Name:	Meyer Suchowljansky
Benjamin "Benny", "Bugsy" Siegel	
Joseph "Doc" Stacher:	Born: 1902, Israel
	Arrived: U.S.A. 1912
	Deported: To Israel 1964
	Died: 1977
Jacob "Jake" Lansky:	Born: 1904
	Died: September 1983

Samuel "Red" Levine
Irving "Taboo" Sandler,
Cousin of Lansky
Harry "Big Greenie" Greenberg: Murdered:
                                    November 22, 1939

Moe "Dimples" Wolensky: Murdered: 1942
Gus Greenbaun: Murdered:
                                    October 3, 1958

Benny Siegelbaum: Died: 1984
Phillip "Little Farvel" Kovolick:
Louis "Shadows" Kravitz
Moe Sedway – Real Name: Morris Sedwitz
John Pullman (Later Meyer's man in Chicago)
Harry Teitelbaum   Irving Zwillman
Abner Zwillman   Cuddy Cutlow
Yudie Albert   Meyer Albert
Dutch Goldberg   Daniel Ahearn
Meyer Wessel   Yiddy Bloom
Hymie "Curly" Holtz   Irving Devine
                      Ed Levinson

MURDER INCORPORATED

MURDER INCORPORATED

Formerly Known As:
The Brownsville Gang & The Amboy Dukes
Formed Around 1934

Lepke's Personal Gang
Louis "Lepke" Buchalter, executed April 4, 1944
Benjamin "Bugsy" Siegel, murdered June 20, 1947
Albert Anastasia, murdered October 25, 1957
Louis Capone, no relation to Al Capone, executed April 4, 1944
Emanuel "Mendy" Weiss, executed April 4, 1944
Martin "Buggsy" Goldstein, executed June 12, 1941
Harry "Pittsburgh Phil" Strauss, executed June 12, 1941
Frank "Dasher" Abbandando, executed February 19, 1942
Harry "Happy" Maione, executed February 19, 1942
Charles "The Bug" Workman, spent 23 years in prison
Jacob "Gurrah" Shapiro spent 11 years and died in prison in 1947
Tootsie Feinstein, murdered
Abraham "Bo" Weinberg, murdered September 1934
George DeFeo, murdered June 11, 1930
Anthony Romero, murdered
Jimmy "Dizzy" Feraco, murdered
Abe "Kid Twist" Reles, Born 1910, murdered November 12, 1941

Vito "Chicken Head" Gurino
Seymour "Blue Jaw" Magoon
Joe "The Baker" Liberito
Dandy Jack Parisi
Paul Berger
Louis Stark
John Paul "Frankie" Carbo
Solly Gross
Abraham "Pretty" Levine
Irving "Knadles" Nitzberg
Benny Harris
Jacob Katzenberg
Albert "Allie" Tannenbaum
Jack "Cuppie" Migden

FIRST NEW YORK FAMILY IN MANHATTAN

MORELLO FAMILY

(EVENTUALLY TO BE NAMED GENOVESE FAMILY)

1st NEW YORK FAMILY, MANHATTAN

MORELLO FAMILY
From Corleone Sicily
BLACK HANDERS

Boss- Antonio Morello (brother)
Reign: 1890's to early 1900's

Boss- Giuseppe "Joe" Morello (brother)
Co-Boss- Ignazio "Lupo the Wolf" Saietta (brother-in law in the Morello Family)
Born: 1877 – Arrived in USA 1898
Reign: early 1900's to 1910
Both Giuseppe and Ignazio went to prison in 1910
Ignazio released 1920
Ignazio went back to Sicily in 1921—1922
Ignazio died in Brooklyn 1944

Boss- Niccolo "Nick" Morello (brother)
Born: 1866
Reign: 1910—1916
He tried to organize Manhattan Sicilian Mafia with Brooklyn Neopolitan Camorra
Murdered: 1916

Boss- Ciro "The Artichoke King" Terranova
(brother-in-law in the Morello Family)
Born: 1881
Reign: 1916—1918
Steps down for nephew Peter Morello
Died: 1938

Boss- Pietro "Peter" "The Clutching Hand" Morello
(nephew)
Born: 1880
Reign: 1918—1922
Murdered: August 15, 1930

TURNING POINT IN MANHATTAN ALONE

From 1920 there were in Manhattan 5 major Italian groups and 1 major Jewish group of the garment district, Lower Eastside.

REINA GROUP	MASSERIA GROUP	MORELLO GROUP
Gaetano Reina	Giuseppe Masseria	Pietro Morello
Ally to Masseria	In 1922 Masseria at	In 1922 Morello
	The top of a large	merges with
	Group with Reina	Masseria
	Group as an ally.	as 1 group.

MAURO GROUP	VALENTI GROUP	JEWISH GROUP
Salvatore Mauro,	Umberto Valenti,	Jacob Orgen,
Murdered 1921	"Lo Spirito"	"Little Augie"
by Masseria forces.	Murdered 1922	1923 Orgen
Members join	by Masseria forces.	murders
Masseria group	Members join	"Kid Dropper"
	Masseria group	Kaplan
		and controls
		garment district

By 1923 in Manhattan there are 2 Italian groups, Reina and Masseria and 1 Jewish group, Orgen.

1st NEW YORK FAMILY

MANHATTAN

Boss-	Giuseppe "Joe The Boss" Masseria Born: 1880 Arrived from Sicily 1903 Merged with Pietro Morello 1922 and became Boss Reign: 1922—April 1931 Opposed Salvatore Maranzano in the Castellamare War 1928—1931 Murdered: April 15, 1931 by Luciano forces
Underboss-	Giuseppe "Joe Baker" Catania, murdered: February 3, 1931
Underboss-	Charles "Lucky" Luciano
Consigliere-	Pietro "The Clutching Hand" Morello, murdered: August 15, 1930 by Luciano forces
Boss-	Charles "Lucky" Luciano Real Name: Salvatore Lucania Born: November 24, 1897; Lercara Friddi, Sicily Arrives in U.S.A. 1906 Two brothers (Giuseppe & Bartolo)

Founder of The National Crime Syndicate
Grows up in Lower Eastside
Forms his own little gang in 1912
Meets Frank Costello 1913
Meets Lansky & Siegel 1913
Merges both gangs 1915
Costello joins 1918
Joe Adonis joins 1920
Luciano joins Joe Masseria gang 1928
He forms "Group Seven" 1928:
1) It consists of 3 Italians from Manhattan- Luciano, Costello and Torrio now living in New York.
2) Two Jews from Manhattan—Lansky & Siegel.
3) One Italian from Brooklyn- Adonis.
4) One Jew and 2 Italians from North Jersey- Longie Zwillman, Willie Moretti and Ruggiero Boiardo.
5) One Englishman from Atlantic City Nocky Johnson.
6) One Jew from Boston—King Soloman.
7) Four Jews from Philadelphia- Max "Boo Boo" Hoff,
Bitzy Bitz, Nig Rosen, Waxey Gordon.
And that's how they got the name from 7 areas.
Reign: April 1931—March 1947
Convention for Luciano in Congress Hotel in Chicago October 1931.
Formed a seven man commission, each head of the 5 different New York family's and 1 from Buffalo and 1 from Chicago from 1931—1956, in 1956 two more cities were added to the commission, Detroit and Philadelphia.

The Genealogy of American Organized Crime [55]

Started a branch of his family in northern New Jersey with one of Lansky's men, Abner Zwillman and one of his own men Willie Moretti.
One of the organizers of the 1929 Atlantic City Crime Convention.
Imprisoned: June 18, 1936.
Deported: February 9, 1946 to Italy.
Arrives in Cuba October 1946
Deported from Cuba to Italy 1947.
Is on $25,000 a month pension from his family while in Italy.
Died: January 26, 1962 in Naples, Italy.

Partner & Advisor-	Meyer Lansky
Partner-	Joseph Adonis—and later assigned as Consigliere for Albert Anastasia
Consigliere-	Frank Costello
Underboss-	Vito Genovese
Statesman-	Johnny Torrio for Luciano's family

1st NEW YORK FAMILY

MANHATTAN

Meyer "The Little Man" Lansky
Real Name: Maier Suchowljansky
Advisor and Investor
Born: 1902 Grodno, Poland on the Russian border
Arrives in U.S.A. 1911
Brother Jake Lansky born 1904
Meets Bugsy Siegel 1912
Forms Bugs and Meyer gang 1914
One of the organizers of "Group Seven" 1928
One of the organizers of the National Crime Convention in Atlantic City 1929
Delegate to the 1932 Presidential Democratic Convention in Chicago
Helps form National Crime Convention at the Waldorf Astoria, April 1934
Starts to go to Miami and Cuba mid 1930's
Meeting in Cuba with Fulgencio Batista, brings along his attorney Richard Nixon 1941
Forms Crime Convention in Cuba to reinstate Luciano at the top. In October 1946. Entertainer Frank Sinatra in attendance.
Started the Flamingo Casino in Las Vegas with Bugsy Siegel and others in 1946
Moves permanently to Miami in 1953

Starts gambling in Hallandale, Florida in the 1950's with Costello, Adonis and others.
Moves to Israel in 1970
Joins Joseph "Doc" Stacher who had been deported earlier to Israel.
Returns to Miami November 5, 1972.
Dies in Miami January 28, 1983

Benjamin "Bugsy" Siegel
Born: 1905 New York
Parents from Kiev
Forms gang with Lansky 1914
Goes to Los Angeles 1937
Opens Flamingo Casino in Las Vegas, December 26, 1946
Host of opening night is actor George Raft
Entertainer – Jimmy Durante
Band Leader – Xavier Cugot
Murdered: June 20, 1947

1st NEW YORK FAMILY

MANHATTAN

Joe Adonis – "Joey A"
Real Name: Giuseppe Doto
Born: November 22, 1902 Montemarano, Italy
Arrived in U.S.A. 1906
Formed the Broadway Mob
Joins Luciano, Costello, Lansky and Siegel 1920
By mid to late 1920's moves to Brooklyn
Becomes member of the D'Aquilla-Yale group
Opens Joe's Italian Kitchen Restarante catering to politicians such as William O'Dwyer and many others
Close associates "Don Cheech" Scalise and "Little Augie" Pisano
Starts to go to New Jersey in 1937 upon the disbanding of the Newark, N.J. Gaspar D'Amico family
His associate in N.J., Willie Moretti
Assigned by Luciano and Costello as Consigliere to Anastasia in Brooklyn to keep Anastasia in toe.
Consigliere to Costello
The only man to belong to two different families (Luciano & Anastasia Families) and one of the top men of the N.J. Branch of the Luciano Family
Moves to Cliffside Park, N.J. in 1944 permanently
Opens up a restaurant called "Dukes"
Imprisoned: 1951; Released: 1953
Deported: January 3, 1956
Died: Milan, Italy 1972

1st NEW YORK FAMILY

MANHATTAN

Boss- Frank Costello "The Prime Minister"
Real Name: Francesco Castiglia
Born: January 26, 1891; Lauropoli, Calabria
Arrives in Harlem, New York   1895
Acting Boss while Luciano is in prison 1936 1947
Reigned as Boss 1947—1957; Retired
Went to prison 1915, released 1916
Helps form "Group Seven" 1928
Helps form National Crime Convention in Atlantic City in 1929
Goes to the Presidential Democratic Convention in Chicago 1932
Known as "The Fixer" between politicians and the underworld
Helps form National Crime Convention in New York 1934
Goes to New Orleans 1934, operates gambling and slot machines
Associated with this were Governor Huey "Kingfish" Long and Sam Carolla of Louisiana
Left in charge of his enterprises in Louisiana is his brother-in-law,

Associates-	Dudley Geigerman, Seymour Weiss and Dandy Phil Kastel Born: 1886; Suicide: 1962 Costello's gambling czar in Miami Frank Erickson (cousin to Owney Madden), Born: 1896; Died: March 2, 1968 Costello's older brother Eduardo, born: 1886 William "Big Bill" Dwyer, born: 1883; career peak 1925, Mayor William O"Dwyer, Congressman Vito Marcantonio, Judge Frances X. Mancuso, District Attorney William Dodge, Judge Thomas Aurelio, Mayor Jimmy Walker, Governor Al Smith (lost to Herbert Hoover in the 1928 Presidential election), Hugo Rogers, Selah Strong, Jim Farley, Jimmy Hines, Al Marinelli, Carmine DeSapio, John Curry and Richard Croker the Tammany Hall Boss Was the main character for the 1950—1951 Senator Kefauver T.V. committee hearings Costello shot in the head and survived May 2, 1957 by Genovese's gunmen Vincent Gigante Retired: 1957 Died 1973 His grave was bombed 7 years after his death
Underboss-	Willie Moretti, murdered October 24, 1951
Underboss-	Michele "Trigger Mike" Coppola, Born: 1904; died 1966
Consigliere-	Joe Adonis
Advisor & Partner-	Meyer Lansky

1st NEW YORK FAMILY

MANHATTAN
REFERRED TO FROM NOW ON AS THE GENOVESE FAMILY

Boss-   Vito "Don Vitone" Genovese
Born: November 27, 1897; Rosiglano, Italy
Arrives in U.S.A. 1913
Brother Michele
Namesake of this family from this time on by the media
Flees to Italy 1937
Associated while in Italy with Benito Mussolini
Ran Black Market and narcotics while in Italy
Returns to U.S.A. in 1944
Imprisoned 1944 and released July 1946
Reign: 1957—1969
Called together the Apalachin Convention November 24, 1957
Imprisoned 1959
Died in prison 1969

Underboss-   Tony Bender; Real Name: Anthony Strollo
Born: June 18, 1899
Murdered: April 8, 1962

Consigliere- & Underboss-   Michele "Big Mike" Miranda
Born: July 26, 1897

Consigliere-   Gerardo Catena
Soldier-   Giuseppe "Joe" Valachi
                 Born: 1903
                 Son-in-law to Gaetano Reina
                 Turned States evidence 1963
                 Died in prison 1971

GENOVESE FAMILY
ACTING DUAL BOSSES WHILE GENOVESE IS IN PRISON

New York Portion	New Jersey Portion
Thomas Eboli	Gerardo "Jerry" Catena
Alias Tommy Ryan	Real Name: Gerardo Rullo
Born: 1911	Born: January 8, 1902
Brother: Pasquale	Imprisoned: 1970—1975
	Brother: Eugene "Gino"

REIGNED TOGETHER 1956—1969
Upon the death of Genovese in prison Tommy Eboli took over alone.

Boss-   Tommy Eboli
                 Reign: 1969—1972
                 Murdered: July 6, 1972
Underboss-   Charles "The Blade" Tourine Sr.
                 Born: March 26, 1905
                 Died: 1989
Consigliere-   Filippo "Cockeyed Phil"
                 Lombardo
                 Died: 1981

Boss-   Francesco "Frank", "Funzi" Tieri
                 Born: 1904 Castelgandolfo, Italy
                 Arrives in U.S.A 1911
                 Reign: 1972—1981
                 Died: March 1981

Underboss-	Carmine "Eli" Zeccardi, Murdered
Underboss-	Matthew "Matty The Horse" Ianniello
	Born: 1929
Consigliere-	Antonio "Buckaloo" Ferro
Consigliere-	Filippo "Cockeyed Phil", "Benny The Squint" Lombardo
Boss-	Anthony "Fat Tony" Salerno
	Born: August 5, 1911
	Reign: 1981—1987
	Went to prison 1987
	Died in prison July 1992
	Three brothers Angelo, Ferdinand and Cirino "Speed" Salerno
Underboss-	Louis "The Gimp" Avitabile
	Born: June 13, 1911
Underboss-	Vincent "The Chin" Gigante
Consigliere-	Filippo Lombardo
Capo in NJ-	Anthony "Tony Pro" Provenzano
	Died in prison
	Two Brothers: Sam and Nunzio
Boss-	Vincent "The Chin" Gigante
	Born: March 29, 1926
	Reign: 1987—1994
	Imprisoned: 1997
	Brothers Mario, Ralph, Louis and 2 others
Underboss-	Michael Generoso
	Born: 1918
Underboss-	Venero "Benny Eggs" Mangano
	Born: September 7, 1921
Underboss-	Saverio "Sammy" Santora
	Born: June 6, 1935
	Died: May 28, 1987
Underboss-	Liborio "Barney" Bellono

Consigliere-	Louis "Bobby" Manna (New Jersey Fraction), Imprisoned
	Born: December 2, 1929
Capo-	Alfonse "Alie Shades" Malangone
	Born: 1936
Acting Boss-	Mario Gigante (brother)
	Born: ?
	Reign: 1994-?
Underboss-	Paul "Slick" Geraci
Consigliere-	James Ida
	Born: 1938

SECOND NEW YORK FAMILY

REINA FAMILY

(EVENTUALLY TO BE NAMED LUCHESE FAMILY)

2nd NEW YORK FAMILY

BRONX & MANHATTAN

Boss-	Gaetano "Tom" Reina Born: 1889 Reign: ? – 1930 Ally to Joe Masseria Murdered: February 26, 1930
Boss-	Giuseppe "Joe" Pinzolo Appointed by Joe Masseria Reign: March 1930—September 1930 Murdered: September 1930
Boss-	Gaetano "Tom" Gagliano Appointed by Salvatore Maranzano Reign: April 1931—1953 Died: 1953
Underboss-	Thomas Lucchese
Consigliere-	?
Top Capo-	Dominic "The Gap" Petrilli Goes to Italy for several years and returns Murdered: December 9, 1953
Boss-	Gaetano "Tommy", "Three Fingers Brown" Lucchese Namesake of this family from this time on by the media Born: December 1, 1899

	Arrived in U.S.A. 1911
	Reign: 1953—1967
	Associated closely with Lucky Luciano and Frank Costello
	Died: July 13, 1967
	Two brothers Joseph & James
Underboss-	Stefano Rondelli
Consigliere-	Vincenzo Rao
	Born: April 27, 1907
Boss-	Carmine Tramunti
	Reign: 1967—1974
	Went to prison 1974
	Died in prison 1978
Underboss-	Stefano La Salle
Consigliere-	Vincenzo Rao
	Born: April 27, 1907
Boss-	Antonio "Tony Ducks" Corollo
	Born: January 12, 1914
	Reign: 1974—1987
	Went to prison 1987
Underboss-	Salvatore "Tom Mix" Santoro
	Born: November 18, 1915
Consigliere-	Christopher Furnari
	Born: April 30, 1924
Acting Boss-	Alfonse D'Arco
	Born: 1933
	Reign: 1987—1988
	Imprisoned, turned state evidence
Acting Underboss-	Aniello Migliore
Acting Consigliere-	Anthony "Gas Pipe" Casso
Boss-	Victorio "Vic" Amuso
	Born: November 4, 1934
	Reign: 1988—1994

	Imprisoned: June 15, 1992
Underboss-	Anthony "Gas Pipe" Casso
	Born: May 21, 1940
	Imprisoned, turned state evidence
Consigliere-	Mariano Macaluso
	Born: June 6, 1912
Capo-	Pete Chiodo, survived murder attempt
	Born: 1941
Capo-	Anthony Perna
	Imprisoned: 1990
Boss-	Joseph Defede
	Born: 1934
	Reign: 1994—?
Underboss-	Steven Crea
	Born: 1948
Consigliere-	?

THIRD NEW YORK FAMILY

(FIRST IN BROOKLYN)

D'AQUILLA FAMILY

(EVENTUALLY TO BE NAMED GAMBINO FAMILY)

3rd FAMILY IN NEW YORK
(1st FAMILY IN BROOKLYN)

With the Grand Master of the Camorra, Enrico Alfano having gone to prison in 1911 and his successor, Pelligrino Marano, going to prison in 1917, the Camorra was then headed by Alexandro Vollero. Under his leadership it fell apart and finally disbanded.

By 1923 members joined either of these two groups regardless if they were Neapolitans or from any other part of Italy, the D'Aquilla group or Schirio group.

Also in 1923, in Brooklyn, there was one Irish waterfront group, "The White Hand Gang".

WESTSIDE WATERFRONT IRISH GROUP
THE WHITE HAND GANG
REIGN: EARLY 1900—1928

Boss-   Dennis "Dinny" Meehan
         Reign: ?—1920
         Murdered: 1920

Boss-   William "Wild Bill" Lovett
         Born: 1892
         Reign: 1920—1923
         Murdered: October 31, 1923 by the D'Aquilla forces

Boss-   Richard "Pegleg" Lonergan

Reign: 1923—1925
Murdered: on Christmas, December 25, 1925 by Al Capone

Boss- John "Cockeye" Dunn
Reign: 1925—1928
Gang now disbanded and members joined Al Mineo group
Executed: 1949
Other members of the White Hand gang through the years 1918—1928:

Joseph "Irish Eyes" Duggan	Murdered: 1921
Edward "Charleston Eddie" McFarland	Murdered: 1921
Edward "Pug" McCarthy	Murdered: 1921
Daniel Bean	Murdered: 1920
Peter Bean	Murdered: 1922
Joseph Bean	Murdered: 1923
James "The Bug" Callaghan	Murdered: 1923
John "Needles" Ferry	Murdered: December 25, 1925
Aaron Harms	Murdered: 1925
Joseph "Ragtime" Howard	Murdered: December 25, 1925
Patrick "Happy" Maloney	Murdered: 1925
Wallace "The Squint" Walsh	Murdered: June 19, 1925

Ernie "Shinny" Shea	Ernie "Scarecrow" Monaghan
James "No Heart" Hart	John "Square Face" Finnegan
Frank "Ash Can" Smitty	Harry "The Fart" O'Toole
Edward Lynch	Garry Barry

3rd FAMILY ITALIAN GROUP BROOKLYN AND THE EASTSIDE WATERFRONT

(Eventually to be named Gambino Family)

Boss-	Salvatore "Toto" D'Aquilla
	Born: Sicily
	Reign: ?—1928
	Sought to be Capo Di Tutti Caprí
	Murdered: October 10, 1928
Associate-	Frankie Yale
	Real Name: Francesco Uale
	Born: 1885
	President of the National Union Siciliano
	Murdered: July 1, 1928 by Capone forces
	Brother Antonio Uale
Other Associates-	Paolo "Paul Kelly" Vaccarelli, Guglielmo "Dui Cuteddi", "Willie" Altierri, Augie Pisano, Joe Adonis, Vincenzo "Jimmy" Crissall and Joe Profaci who breaks away from this group in 1928 to start his own group.
Boss-	Al Mineo
	Real Name: Alfredo Manfredi
	Appointed to this position by Joe Masseria
	Reign: 1928—1930
	Murdered: November 5, 1930
Underboss-	Stefano Ferrigno

	Murdered: November 5, 1930
	Both murdered by Maranzano and Profaci forces
Boss-	Vincenzo "Vince" Mangano
	Born: 1888
	Arrives in U.S.A. 1922
	Appointed by Maranzano to this position
	Reign: April 1931—1951
	Murdered: April 1951
Underboss-	Filippo "Phil" Mangano
	Brother to Vincenzo Mangano
	Murdered: 1951
Consigliere-	Francesco "Don Cheech" Scalise
Boss-	Albert Anastasia
Real Name:	Umberto Anastasio
	Born: 1903
	Arrives in U.S.A. around 1918
	8 Brothers
	Reign: 1951—1957
	Close relationship with Luciano, Costello and Adonis
	Murdered: October 25, 1957 by Genovese forces
Underboss-	Francesco "Frank" "Don Cheech" Scalise
	Born: 1894
	Murdered: July 1957
	Brother Giuseppe "Joe" Scalise murdered August 1957
Consigliere & Advisor-	Joe Adonis
	Appointed by Luciano to this position
	Deported January 3, 1956
Capo-	Antonio "Tough Tony" Anastasio Brother of Albert Anastasia

	Born: 1906
	Died: 1963
Capo-	John "Johnny Dio" Dioguardi
	Born: 1915
	Went to prison 1973 Died in prison 1979
Capo-	Anthony "Little Augie" Pisano
	Real Name: Anthony Carfano
	Murdered: September 29, 1959
Boss-	Carlo Gambino
	Born: 1902, Palermo, Sicily
	Arrives in U.S.A. 1921
	Namesake of this family from this time on by the media
	Brother Paul Gambino
	Reign: October 1957—October 1976
	Died: October 1976
Underboss -	Joseph "Bandy " Biondo 1957—1965
Underboss -	Aniello Dellacroce
	Born: 1914
	Died: December 2, 1985
Consigliere-	Joseph Riccobono
Advisor-	Carmine "The Doctor" Lambardozzi
	Born: February 13, 1913
Capo -	Joseph Paterno in New Jersey around the 1970's.
Boss-	Paul "Big Paul" Castellano
	Brother-in-law to Carlo Gambino
	Born: 1915
	Reign: 1976—1985
	Murdered: December 16, 1985
Underboss & Statesman-	Aniello Dellacroce
	Died: December 2, 1985
Underboss-	Thomas Bilotti

	Born: 1940
	Murdered: December 16, 1985
Consigliere-	Joseph N. Gallo
	Born: 1914
Capo-	James "Jimmy Brown" Failla
	Born: January 1919
Boss-	John Gotti
	Born: October 1940
	4 Brothers, Pete, Gene, and 2 others
	Reign: January 1986—April 1992
	Imprisoned: 1992
Underboss-	Frank DeCicco
	Born: November 5, 1935
	Murdered: April 13, 1986
Acting	
Underboss-	Angelo Ruggiero
	Born: 1940
	Died: December 6, 1989
Underboss-	Joe "Piney" Armone
	Born: September 3, 1917
	Died in prison
Acting	
Underboss-	John "The Nose" D'Amico
	Born: July 9, 1934
Consigliere	
& Underboss-	Salvatore "Sammy The Bull" Gravano
	Born: March 12, 1945
	Imprisoned 1992, Turned state evidence
Consigliere-	Frank "Frankie Loc" Locascio
	Born: September 24, 1932
	Imprisoned with John Gotti in 1992
Acting Boss-	Giuseppe "Joe" Arcui
	Born: September 22, 1913
	Reign: April 1992—1996

Acting Underboss-	Daniel Marino
	Born: January 7, 1940
Capo-	Nicholas Corozzo
	Born: 1940
Capo-	Robert Basichia of Belvedere, New Jersey
Acting Boss-	Nicholas "Little Guy" Corozzo
	Born: January 7, 1940
	Reign: November 1996—1998
	Arrested: January 1998
Capo-	Leonard DiMaria
	Born: 1941
Boss-	Greg DePalma
	Born: ?
	Reign: 1998—?

FOURTH NEW YORK FAMILY

SCHIRIO FAMILY

(EVENTUALLY TO BE NAMED BONANNO FAMILY)

4th NEW YORK FAMILY BROOKLYN

EVENTUALLY TO BE KNOWN AS THE BONANNO FAMILY

Boss- Nicholo Schirio
Born: Palermo, Sicily
Reign: ?—1928
Stepped down for Salvatore Maranzano in 1928
Died

Boss- Salvatore "Tuiddu" Maranzano in 1928
Born: 1868, Castellammare Del Golfo, Sicily
Came to U.S.A. for Don Vito Cascio Ferro in 1918, 1925 and 1927
Reign: 1928—September 1931
Upon the murder of Masseria gave himself a banquet at The Grand
Concourse in the Bronx for all New York families in April 1931
In May of 1931 gave himself a National Banquet Convention in
Wappingers Falls, New York and appointed himself Capo Di Tutti Capri (Boss of Bosses)
Top Man during the Castellammare War, (April

15, 1928—April 15, 1931)
Appointed the Heads of the other 4 families
Murdered: September 11, 1931 by Luciano forces
Underboss- Angelo Caruso

REFFERRED TO FROM NOW ON AS THE BONANNO FAMILY

Boss- Giuseppe "Joseph" Bonanno
Alias Joe Bananas
Namesake of this family from now on by the media
Born: 1905, Castellammare Del Golfo, Sicily
Came to U.S.A., New York 1906
Returned 1911 to Sicily
Arrived again in Tampa, Florida, December 1924 with Cousin
Antonino Magaddino
Reign: September 1931—1964
Deposed by the Commission 1964
Retired to Tucson, Arizona 1964
Underboss- Francesco "Frank" Garofalo
Between 1931—1956
Retired to Sicily
Underboss- Carmine Galante
Between 1956—1962
Imprisoned
Underboss- John Morale
Between 1962—1964
Consigliere- John Tartamelo
Consigliere- John Bonventre

Boss- Gaspar DiGregorio
Brother-in-law to Stefano Magaddino
Reign: 1964 -1966
Steps down

	Died: 1968
Underboss-	Paolo "Paul" Sciacca
Boss-	Paolo "Paul" Sciacca
	Reign: 1966—1970
	Steps down
	Died later the same year 1970
Underboss-	Peter Crociata
Consigliere-	Joseph DeFillippi
Boss-	Natale Evola
	Reign: 1970 -1973 Died: 1973
Underboss-	John "Big John" Ormento, Died in prison 1974
Consigliere-	Philip Rastelli
Boss-	Philip "Rusty" Rastelli
	Reign: 1973 -1974
	Steps down for Galante who was released from prison
Underboss-	Pietro Licata, murdered 1976
Underboss-	Joseph DeFillippo
Boss-	Carmine "The Cigar" "Lillo" Galante
	Born: 1910
	Reign: 1974—1979
	Imprisoned: 1962—1974
	Murdered: July 1979
Underboss-	Nicholas Marangelo
	Born: July 13, 1912
Consigliere	Stefano Cannone
	Died 1985
Boss-	Philip "Rusty" Rastelli
	Born: January 31, 1918
	Reign: 1979—1988

	Imprisoned: 1987
	Died in prison 1991
Underboss-	Salvatore "Toto" Catalano
	Born: February 24, 1941
	Arrives in U.S.A. 1966 for the Sicilian Connection
	Imprisoned: 1987
Underboss-	Joseph Massina
	Born: January 10, 1943
Consigliere-	Salvatore "Sally Fruits" Ferrugia
	Born: January 19, 1914
	Acting boss in 1989
Consigliere-	Joseph Buccellato
	Born: July 16, 1919
Consigliere-	Anthony Spero
	Born: February 18, 1929
Boss-	Joseph Massina
	Born: January 10, 1943
	Reign: 1990—?
Underboss-	Salvatore Vitale
	Born: 1948
Consigliere-	James Tartaglione
	Born: 1937

FIFTH NEW YORK FAMILY

PROFACI FAMILY

(EVENTUALLY TO BE NAMED COLOMBO FAMILY)

5th NEW YORK FAMILY BROOKLYN AND STATEN ISLAND

EVENTUALLY TO BE KNOWN AS THE COLOMBO FAMILY

Boss-   Rafaele Palizzola
        Black Hander in Brooklyn
        Born: Sicily
        Reign: around 1908

CAMORRA—ORIGIN NAPLES, ITALY

Boss-   Enrico Alfano, (Grand Master)
        Reign: ?—1911
        Went to prison 1911

Boss-   Pelligrino Morano
        Reign: 1911—1917
        Goes to prison in 1917

Boss-   Alessandro Vollero
        Reign: 1917—?
        This is the beginning of the end of the Camorra under his leadership the Camorra fell apart and members joined other Italian groups.

SICILIAN GROUP
A SPLINTER GROUP FROM THE D'AQUILA-YALE GROUP

Boss-	Giuseppe "Peppino" "Joe" Profaci
	Born: 1896
	Arrived from Castellammara Del Golfo, Sicily 1922
	Reign: 1928—1962
	Died: 1962
	Brothers Salvatore and Francesco
Underboss-	Giuseppe "Joseph" Magliocco

A 2nd FRACTION
THE GALLO BROTHERS GROUP
Larry Gallo, Died June 6th 1968
Joseph "Crazy Joe" Gallo, Born: 1929; Murdered: April 8, 1972
Albert "Kid Blast" Gallo and Others

Boss-	Giuseppe "Joseph" Magliocco
	Born: 1898, Castellammare Del Golfo, Sicily
	Arrives U.S.A. 1926
	Reign: 1962—1963
	Died: December 28, 1963
	Brother Antonio, Born 1908
Underboss-	Salvatore "Sally The Sheik" Mussachio
Consigliere-	Ambrose Magliocco
	Born: January 1, 1901

COLOMBO FAMILY

Boss-	Joseph Colombo
	Born: 1914
	Namesake of this family from this time on by the media
	Appointed by Carlo Gambino to this leadership
	Reign: January 1964—June 1971

	Founder of The Italian American Civil Rights League
	Shot: June 1971, in coma for 7 years
	Died: 1978
Underboss-	Salvatore C. Mineo
	Born: 1897
Underboss-	Anthony "Abbie Shots" Abbattemarco
Consigliere-	Joseph Yacovelli
	Born: January 14, 1928
Boss-	Tomaso DiBello
	Born: November 29, 1905
	Reign: 1971—1981
	Stepped down for a younger man
Underboss-	Anthony Abbattemarco
	Born: April 1922
Consigliere-	Alfonso Persico Sr.
Boss-	Carmine "Junior" Persico
	Born: August 8, 1931
	Reign: 1981—1987
	Goes to prison 1987
Underboss-	John "Sonny" Franzese
	Born: February 1919
	Imprisoned
Underboss-	Gennaro "Jerry Lang" Langella
	Born: December 30, 1938
	Imprisoned
Consigliere-	Alfonso Persico Sr.
	Born: December 6, 1929
	Brother to Carmine Persico
	Imprisoned
Consigliere-	Carmine Sessa
Acting Boss-	Anthony "Scappy" Scarpati
	Reign: 1987—1988

Boss-	Victor Orena
	Born: August 4, 1934
	Reign: 1988—1992
	Imprisoned: 1992
Underboss-	William Cutola—Murdered
Underboss-	Pasquale Amato
	Born: July 3, 1934
Underboss-	Benedetto Aloi
	Born: October 6, 1935
Underboss-	Joseph Russo
	Born: August 14, 1953
Consigliere-	Frank Melli
	Born: December 16, 1941
Capo—	Alphonse Persico (Son of Carmine Persico)
Advisor-	Michael Franzese
	Given Name: Michael Grillo
	Born: May 17, 1951
	Imprisoned
Boss-	Andrew Russo
	Born: 1934
	Reign: 1993—?
Underboss-	Joel Cacace
	Born: 1941
Consigliere-	Vincenzo Aloi
	Born: 1933

THE NEW JERSEY FAMILY

NEW JERSEY GROUPS

THE REINFIELD SYNDICATE STARTED IN NEW YORK IN 1910 THEN MOVED TO

NORTHERN NEW JERSEY

Boss-   Joseph Reinfield
Formed in the early 1900's in New York
A member from the old Bugs and Meyers gang in New York, "Longie Zwillman" now joins Reinfield in New Jersey.
Joined later by Willie Moretti, Joe Adonis and Ruggiero Boiardo.

NEWARK, NEW JERSEY FAMILY

Boss—   Stefano Badami
Reign: ? – 1931
Underboss— Salvatore Monaco
Murdered. 1931

Boss-   Gaspar D'Amico
Reign: 1931—1937

Shot and wounded February 22, 1937
Goes back to Sicily at that time
Family disbands
Members go to either New Jersey branch of
Costello Family with
Willie Moretti or Elizabeth, New Jersey Family

NORTHERN NEW JERSEY SYNDICATE
INDEPENDENT AND YET AFFILIATED WITH LUCIANO FAMILY
THROUGH MEYER LANSKY

Boss- Abner "Longie" Zwillman
Born: 1899
Reign: after Joe Reinfield
Associated closely with Meyer Lansky
Known as Capone of New Jersey
Connections with many New Jersey politicians
Suicide: February 27, 1959
Brother Irving Zwillman
Associates- Maxey Greenberg, Arnold Rothstein, Waxey Gordon
At various times in the 1920's
Partner- Ruggiero "Richie The Boot" Boiardo
Born: 1891
Arrives in U.S.A. 1900
Died: November 1984
Underboss- Quarico "Willie" Moretti
Born: 1894
Moretti and Adonis move in on Gaspar D'Amico in 1937
Murdered: October 25, 1951
Underboss- Michele "Mike" Lascari
Consigliere- Joe Adonis
The only person to belong to 2 families,
The Luciano Family and The Anastasia Family

One of the top men in the New Jersey branch of the Costello Family
Moves into New Jersey permanently in 1944

Boss- Michele "Mike" Lascari
 Reign: 1955—?
Underboss- Angelo Lapadura
Underboss- Jerry Catena
Consigliere- Joe Adonis
Consigliere- Ruggiero Boiardo
Capo- Angelo "Ray" "The Gyp" DeCarlo Died: 1973
Capo- Anthony "Little Pussy" Russo Murdered

Boss- Jerry Catena
 Reign: Mid 1960's—1971
Capo- John DiGilio, Mid 1980's, Murdered 1988
Associate- George Weingartner, Mid 1990's, Suicide July 5, 1998

INDEPENDENT GANG
CAMPISI GANG OF NEWARK, NEW JERSEY
NOT RECOGNIZED BY ORGANIZED CRIME

Gang
Members: Made up of Brothers, Cousins, Brother-in laws, Nephews and a very few close friends. Vincent, Anthony, Carmen, Peter S., Peter C., Salvatore, Biaggio and Thomas Peter Campisi
Started around 1968
In 1973 many were imprisoned and eventually released.

ELIZABETH, NEW JERSEY FAMILY

Boss- Filippo "Big Phil" Amari
 Reign: ?—1957
 Goes to Italy
 Died: September 24, 1963

Boss-	Nicholo Delmore
	Reign: 1957—1964
	Died: February 2, 1964
Underboss-	Louis LaRasso
Boss-	Simone "Sam The Plumber" DeCavalcante
	Alias: Simone Rizzo
	Born: May 4, 1912
	Reign: 1964—1985 Retired
	Imprisoned: 1972
	4 brothers
	Died: February 7, 1997
Underboss-	Joseph LeSalva (Connecticut)
Underboss-	Frank Majuri
Consigliere-	Steven Vitabile
Associate-	Harold "Kayo" Konigsberg
Boss-	John Riggi
	Born: 1924
	Reign: 1985—?
	Imprisoned: 1990
Underboss-	Vincent Rotondo
Acting boss-	Vincent "Vinny Ocean" Palermo
	Reign: Mid 1990's—?

THE PHILADELPHIA, PA AND SOUTH JERSEY FAMILY

PHILADELPHIA, PA., SOUTHERN NEW JERSEY & ATLANTIC CITY FAMILY

THE BLOODY TUB GANG
Prominent around 1915

TOP BOOTLEGGERS

Max "Boo Boo" Hoff
Reign: 1891—late 1930's
Bitzy Bitz
Waxey Gordon
Harry Stromberg:
Alias Nig Rosen
Sam Lazar
Max Hassell

Willie Weisberg
Mugsy Taylor
Matteo Brothers:
Francesco, Salvatore & Nicholas
Max "Chinkie" Rothman
Samuel "Cappie" Hoffman
Joseph "Little Kirssy" Herman
Charles Schwartz

ITALIAN GROUP

1st Fraction
Boss-Salvatore Sabella
Born: 1891, Sicily
Reign: 1920's—?

2nd Fraction
Pius Lanzetti & 7 Brothers
Musky Zanghi & 2 Brothers
The Morrazzo Brothers

By 1939 Pius and 5 brothers, the Morrazzo brothers, Joe Zanghi and others all murdered. This fraction then disbanded.

Boss: Giovanni "John" Avena

Reign: ?—1936
Murdered: August 1936

Boss: Giuseppe "Peppino" "Joe" Bruno
Based in South Jersey
Reign: 1936—1941 Retired
Died: October 22, 1946
Underboss of
South Jersey &
Atlantic City: Marco Reginelli
Underboss of
Philadelphia: Giuseppe "Joe" Ida

Boss: Giuseppe "Joe" Ida
Reign: 1941—1959
Retired to Sicily
Underboss of
Philadelphia: Antonio Dominic Pollina
Born: 1893
Died: March 1, 1993

Underboss of
South Jersey &
Atlantic City Marco Reginelli
Died: 1956
Consigliere: Dominic Olivetto
Statesman: Giuseppe "Joe" Bruno

Boss: Angelo Bruno
Real Name: Angelo Annaloro
No relation to Joe Bruno
Born: 1910, Villalba, Sicily
Served on Commission at one period
Reign: 1959—1980
Murdered: March 21, 1980
1 Brother, Vito Bruno
Underboss: Ignazio Denano
Died: August 20, 1970

Underboss:	Phillip Testa
Consigliere:	Giuseppe "Joe" Rugnetta
	Died: 1977
Consigliere:	Antonio "Tony Banana" Caponigro
	Murdered: April 18, 1980

Boss:	Phillip "Chicken Man" Testa
	Born: 1924
	Reign: March 1980—March 1981
	Murdered: March 1981
Underboss:	Peter Casella, Died: October 1983
Underboss:	Frank "Chickie" Narducci, Murdered: January 7, 1982
Consigliere:	Nicodemo Scarfo
Capo:	John "Johnny Keys" Simone, Murdered: September 19, 1980
Capo:	Frank Sindone, Murdered: October 29, 1980

Based in Atlantic City

Boss:	Nicodemo "Little Nicky" Scarfo
	Born: 1929
	Reign: 1982-1990
	Imprisoned: 1988

2nd FRACTION-

	Harry "Hunchback" Riccobene
	Born: 1910
	Imprisoned: 1985
	Died in prison: 2000
	2 Brothers
	Mario Riccobene—Imprisoned
	Robert Riccobene—Murdered
Underboss:	Salvatore "Chuckie" Merlino
	Imprisoned: 1988
	Brother Lawrence "Yogi" Merlino
	Imprisoned: 1988
Underboss:	Phillip "Crazy Phil" Leonetti

	Imprisoned: 1988
	Turned state evidence
	Went into Witness Protection Program
	Nephew of Nicky Scarfo
Consigliere:	Frank Monte
	Murdered: May 13, 1982
Consigliere:	Nick "Nicky Buck" Piccolo
Boss:	John Stanfa
	Born: 1941, Palermo, Sicily
	Arrives in U.S.A. 1961
	Driver of Angelo Bruno when Bruno was murdered
	Connected strongly with the Gambino Family and the Sicilian Nimo Group
	Reign: 1991—1995
	Imprisoned for life November 1995
Underboss:	Joseph F. Ciancaglini Jr.
	Born: 1956
	Shot in the head 3 times on March 2, 1993 and survived
Underboss:	Frank Martines
	Born: 1953
	Imprisoned for life November 1995
Consigliere:	Anthony "Tony Buck" Piccolo
	Born: 1922
Capo:	Salvatore "Shotsy" Sparacio
	Born: 1922
	Imprisoned: November 1995
Capo:	Vincent "Al Pajamas" Pagano
	Born: 1929
	Imprisoned: November 1995
Boss:	Ralph Natale
	Born: 1935
	Reign: 1996—?
	Arrested 1999, Turned state evidence

Underboss: Joseph "Skinny Joey" Merlino
              Born: 1962
              Imprisoned: 1999
              Son of Salvatore "Chuckie" Merlino
Consigliere: John "Johnny Chang" Ciancaglini
Consigliere: Ronald Turchi,
              Born: 1938—Murdered: October 24, 1999
Consigliere: George Borgesi
Capo: Steve Mazzone

ATLANTIC CITY POLITICAL POWERS

Political Boss: Louis Kuehnle
              Reign: 1881—1911
              Imprisoned: 1911
              Died: 1934

Boss: Enoch "Nucky" Johnson
              Reign: 1911—1941
              Imprisoned: 1941 for 4 years
              Died: 1969
Associates: Brother Al Johnson
              Herman "Stumpy" Orman

Political Boss: Frank "Hap" Farley (One of the Good Guys)
              Reign: 1941—1971
              Died: 1977

ATLANTIC CITY AND SOUTHERN JERSEY BRANCH OF THE PHILADELPHIA FAMILY

Boss: Marco Reginelli
Reign: 1941—1956
Died: May 25, 1956
Associates during the
1950's & 1960's: Vincent Cammarata
Vincenzo "Jimmy The Brute" DiNatale
During the 1970's:
Ralph Natale
Nicky Scarfo arrives in Atlantic City 1963

THE PITTSTON, PA FAMILY

PITTSTON, PENNSYLVANIA FAMILY

Boss-	Santo "The Old Man" "The Fox" Volpe
	Arrives from Sicily after Stefano LaTorre
	Reign: ?—1940's
	Died
	2 brothers Luigi & Giuseppe Volpe
Underboss-	John Sciandra
Consigliere-	Stefano "Steven" LaTorre
	Born: Montedoro, Sicily
	Arrives from Sicily in 1880
Boss-	John Sciandra
	Reign: 1940's to mid 1950's
Underboss-	Joseph Barbara
Consigliere-	Santo Volpe
Capo-	Joseph Falcone, Sr., Born: January 27, 1902
	Brother Salvatore Falcone
Boss-	Joseph Barbara
	Born: 1905
	Reign: mid 1950's—1959
	Host of the November 24, 1957 Apalachin, NY Crime Convention
	Died: 1959
Underboss-	Russell Bufalino
Consigliere-	Angelo Joseph Sciandra

Boss-   Russell Bufalino
                  Born: 1903, Montedoro, Sicily
                  Reign: 1959—1981
                  Died: 1994
Underboss &
Acting Boss-   Anthony "Guv" Guarnieri
                  Born: 1910
Underboss-   Phillip Medico, Born: 1913
Underboss-   David Osticco, Born: April 22, 1913
Underboss-   William D'Elia
Consigliere-   Edward Sciandra
Capo-   Joseph Falcone, Jr.

Boss-   Edward Sciandra
                  Born: November 13, 1912
                  Reign: 1981—?

Boss-   William D'Elia
                  Reign: 1990's—?

THE BUFFALO, NY FAMILY

BUFFALO, NEW YORK FAMILY

Boss-   Giuseppe "Joe" Peter DiCarlo
             Born: ?
             Reign: ?—1922
             Died: July 9, 1922

Boss-   Stefano Magaddino
             Born: 1891, Castellammare Del Golfo, Sicily
             Arrives in U.S.A. around 1917
             Goes to Buffalo from New York City 1921
             For a while served as Chairman of the Commission
             Worked closely with the Pittston, Pa. family
             Reign: 1922—1969
             Died: July 19, 1974
             Brother Antonino

Underboss-   Federico "The Wolf" Randaccio
             Born: July 24, 1907

Underboss-   Paul Palmeri

Consigliere- Vincent Scro

Capo-   James "Westfield Jimmy" Salamone – Erie, Pa., Convicted: 1961

Capo-   Anthony Ciotti, Convicted: 1970

A SPLINTER GROUP GOES TO ROCHESTER, NY AROUND THIS TIME LATE 1960'S

Acting Boss- Salvatore Pieri
Reign: 1969 – 1970
Imprisoned: 1970 and again in 1978
Died: 1983

2nd FRACTION-

Boss- Joseph Fino
Reign: 1970—1974
Underboss- ?
Consigliere- Salvatore Pieri

Boss- Sam Frangiamore
Reign: 1974—1977
Underboss- ?
Consigliere- ?

Boss- Joseph Todaro Sr.
Born: September 18, 1923
Reign: 1977—?
Underboss- Joseph Anthony Todaro Jr.
Consigliere- Joseph Pieri

THE ROCHESTER, NY FAMILY

THE ROCHESTER, NY FAMILY

ROCHESTER, NEW YORK FAMILY
A BREAK AWAY FROM THE BUFFALO, NY FAMILY

Boss-	Frank Valenti
	Reign: 1960's—1972
	Imprisoned
	Brother Stanley Valenti
Underboss-	Dominic Chirico
	Murdered: June 1972
Underboss-	William Lupo, Murdered—1972
Consigliere-	John Russo
Boss-	Samuel "Red" Russotti
	Born: 1912
	Reign: June 1972—1975
	Imprisoned: 1976—1978
Underboss-	Richard Marino
Consigliere-	Rene Piccarreto
Boss-	Thomas Didio
	Reign: 1975—1978
	Murdered: July 1978

Underboss-	Dominic Celestino
	Murdered: June 1978
Boss-	Samuel "Red" Russotti
	Born: 1912
	Released from prison: 1978
	Reign: 1978—?
Underboss-	Angelo J. Amico
Consigliere-	Rene J. Piccareto
Capo-	Sam Gingello, Born: 1940
Acting Boss-	Thomas Marotta
	Reign: Late 1990's

THE PITTSBURGH, PA FAMILY

PITTSBURGH FAMILY

Boss: Salvatore Calderone
Born: 1858, Sicily
Reign: ?-Late 1931, Retired
Died: 1933

2nd FRACTION-
Stefano Monastero
Murdered: August 6, 1929
Joseph Siragusa
Murdered: September 13, 1931

Boss: Giovanni "John" Bazzano Sr.
Reign: ?—1932
Murdered: August 8, 1932
Underboss: Michael Bua

2nd FRACTION–
The Volpe Brothers
Louis, James, Arthur, John, Joseph and others, most of which were murdered.

Boss: Vincenzo Capizzi
Reign: 1932 -1937
Imprisoned: December 1942

Boss: Frank Amato Sr.
     Born: 1890
     Reign: 1937—1956
Cosigliere: Nicolo Gentile
     Formerly of the Luciano family, goes to
     Sicily, returns and joins the Pittsburgh family

Boss: John S. Larocca
     Born: 1902
     Reign: 1956—1984
     Died: 1984
Underboss: Gabriel "Kelly" Mannarino
     Born: October 1915
     Died: July 11, 1980
Underboss: Michael J. Genovese
Consigliere: Frank Amato Sr.
Consigliere: Anthony Grosso
     Born: 1914
     Imprisoned: 1986
     Died in prison 1994

Boss: Michael James Genovese
     Born: 1920
     Reign: 1984—?
     Cousin to Vito Genovese
Underboss: Joseph Peccora
     Died: March 1987
Underboss: Louis Raucci
     Born: 1931
     Imprisoned: 1990
     Died in prison April 1995
Underboss: John Bazzano Jr.
     Born: 1927
Consigliere: Antonio Ripepi
     Born: July 1902

Capo: Frank Amato Jr.
Capo: Tomaso Ciancutti
Associate: Charles Porter

Affiliate Youngstown, OH BRANCH
Underboss: Leonard Strollo

THE CLEVELAND, OH FAMILY

CLEVELAND FAMILY
MURRAY HILL-MAYFIELD ROAD GANG
ITALIAN SECTION FORMED 1913

Boss- Giuseppe "Big Joe" Lonardo
       Murdered: October 13, 1927
       Giovanni Lonardo
       Murdered: October 13, 1927
       Francesco Lonardo
       Murdered: October 21, 1929

Boss- Giuseppe Porello
       6 other brothers
       Reign: 1927—1929
       Murdered: July 5, 1930

Boss- Salvatore "Black Sam" Todaro
       Murdered: June 6, 1929

CLEVELAND SYNDICATE
FORMED 1926
MERGES WITH ITALIAN FAMILY 1929 IN SOME ENDEAVORS

4 Bosses- Morris Kleinman
           Born: September 19, 1896
           Samuel Tucker
           Born: July 11, 1897
           Morris "Moe" Dalitz
           Born: December 24, 1899

	Died: August 31, 1989
	Louis Rothkopf Alias Lou Rhody
	Born: September 3, 1903
	Suicide
Associates-	Arthur "Mickey" McBride, Born: 1886
	Thomas McGinty, Born: 1892
	Samuel Miller, Gaston B. Means, Jacob Stein
	Convention at Hotel Statler, Cleveland, December 5, 1928. Those in attendance were representatives from New York, NY, Chicago, IL, St. Louis, MO, Tampa Bay, FL, Newark, NJ, Gary, IN, Detroit, MI, and the Italian family of Cleveland, OH
Boss-	Francesco Milano
	Reign: 1929—1935
	Flees to Mexico
	Died: September 15, 1970
	Brothers Anthony Milano and Peter Milano
Boss-	Anthony Milano
	Born: 1898
	Reign: 1935—1940
	Died: August 5, 1978
Boss-	Al "Big Al" Polizzi
	Arrives from Sicily 1900
	Reign: 1940—1953
Underboss-	Charles "Chuck" Polizzi
	Real Name: Leo Berkowitz
	Adopted by the Polizzi family and cousin to Big Al
Consigliere-	Anthony "Tony" Milano
Capos-	Andreola Brothers (John, Frederico & George)
Boss-	John Scalish
	Reign: 1953—1975

	Died: 1976
Underboss-	Joseph DeCarlo
Underboss-	Frank Brancato, Died: 1973
Underboss-	John Angersola
Consigliere-	Tony Milano

Boss-	James "Blackie" Licavoli
Born:	1904
	Reign: 1975—1985
	Imprisoned: 1982
	Died in prison 1985
Underboss-	Leo "The Lip" Moceri, Murdered: September 2, 1976
Underboss-	Angelo Lonardo – Turned state evidence
Underboss-	Tony Liberatore, Imprisoned: 1982
Underboss-	John Calandra, Imprisoned: 1982
Consigliere-	Anthony "Tony Dope" Delsante, Died: August 2, 1977
Consigliere-	John Tronolone

2nd FRACTION-

    Daniel "Danny" Greene, Murdered: October 6, 1977
    John Nardi, Murdered: May 17, 1977

Boss-	John Tronolone
	Born: December 12, 1910
	Reign: 1985—?
	Indited and also died in 1991

INDEPENDENT CINCINNATI BOOTLEGGER ALSO PARTS OF KENTUCKY & INDIANA

Boss-	George Remus
	Born: 1873 in Germany
	Arrives in U.S.A. 1876
	Reign: pre 1924

THE DETROIT, MI FAMILY

DETROIT FAMILY
CLOSE TIES WITH CLEVELAND
& ST. LOUIS FAMILIES

GANGS IN DETROIT AND SOME MEMBERS

PURGE GANG- Started around 1919—1931

PURPLE GANG-
Norman Purple
Abe Bernstein
Joseph Bernstein
Lewis Fleisher
Harry Fleisher
George Lewis
Edward Fletcher

Started around 1919—1931
Morris "Moe" Dalitz
(Goes to Cleveland 1926)
Solly Levine
Harry Keywell
Phillip Keywell
Mert Wertheimer
Samuel Cohen

LITTLE JEWISH NAVY GANG-

"Big Maxey" Greenberg- Formerly of St. Louis. Goes to New York 1920 and joins Arnold Rothstein and Waxey Gordon Murdered: April 12, 1933

ITALIAN GROUP

Boss: Salvatore Catalonette
        Reign: ? –1922
        Died: 1930

Boss-   Gasper Milazzo
        Born: Castellammare Del Golfo, Sicily

	Goes to Detroit from NY 1921
	Reign: 1922—1928
	Murdered: April 15, 1928
	His murder starts the Castellammare War
Underboss-	Santo "Cockeyed Sam" Perrone

2nd FRACTION-

	Caesar LaMare
	Murdered: Feb. 1931
Boss-	Joseph Massei
	Reign: 1928—1950's
Underboss-	Joseph Tocco
	Murdered: May 3, 1938
Underboss-	Peter Licavoli
	Died in Arizona 1984
	Brother Thomas "Yonnie" Licavoli, Imprisoned
Consigliere-	Guglielmo "Black Bill" Tocco
	Born: Terrasina, Sicily
	Died: 1972
Boss-	Joseph Zerilli
	Born: 1897
	Arrives from Terrasina, Sicily 1914
	Reign: 1950's—1977
	Died: October 30, 1977
Underboss-	Giovanni "John" Priziola
	Born: 1895
	Died: April 14, 1979
Underboss-	Angelo Meli
Consigliere-	Dominic "Fats" Corrado
	Brother Paul Corrado
Statesman-	Joseph Massei
Boss-	Jack W. Tocco

Son of "Black Bill" Tocco
Born: 1927
Reign: 1977—?
Arrested: March 14, 1996
Brother Anthony Tocco, Born 1931
Brother Paul J. Tocco, Born 1918
Underboss- Raffaele Quasarano, Born: 1910
Underboss- Mike Polizzi
Underboss- Peter Vitale
Brother Paul Vitale
Cousin Vito Vitale in Sicily
Underboss- Anthony "Tony Jack" Giacalone, Born: 1919,
Arrested: March 14, 1996
Brother Vito "Billy Jack" Giacalone, Born: 1923
Arrested March 14, 1996
Underboss- Anthony Zerilli, Born: 1928
Arrested March 14, 1996
Consigliere- Anthony J. Corrado, Born: 1936
Arrested March 14, 1996
Son of Paul Corrado

JAMES "JIMMY" R. HOFFA
Born: Feb. 14 1913
Former President of the Teamsters Union.
Went to prison 1967, was pardoned by
President Richard Nixon 1971.
On July 30, 1975 A meeting between
Tony Provenzano of the Genovese Family;
head of a North Jersey Union, and Hoffa
was set up by Tony "Jack" Giacaione of Detroit
on orders from Joseph Zerilli of Detroit,
Russell Bufalino of Pittston, PA and
Joe Aiuppa of Chicago. No one showed up
except Hoffa's bodyguard Frank Sheeran,
who was the president of a local union in
Wilmington Delaware, lived in Philadelphia

and was a member of the Pittston, PA mob.
Born 1920 – Died Dec 14, 2003.
Hoffa was never seen again, his body was cremated in a nearby mortuary.

THE MILWAUKEE, WI FAMILY

MILWAUKEE FAMILY

Boss: Vito Guardalabene
Reign: ?—1921
Died: February 6, 1921

Boss: Peter Guardalabene
Son of Vito
Reign: 1921—1924
Died: ?

Boss: Joseph Amato
Reign: 1924—1927
Died: March 28, 1927

Boss: Joseph Vallone
Reign: 1927—1949
Died: March 18, 1952

Boss: Sam Ferrara
Reign: 1949—1952
Retired

Boss: John Alioto
Reign: 1952—1961
Died

Underboss: Giovanni DeBella
Died: 1964

Boss:	Frank P. Balistrieri
	Born: 1918
	Reign: 1961—?
	Imprisoned: 1984
	Died: 1993
	Sons Peter, Joseph & John
Underboss:	Steve DiSalvo
Boss:	Peter F. Balistrieri
	Reign: 1990's—?
	Son of Frank Balistrieri
Underboss:	?
Consigliere:	Joseph Cammeti

AFFILIATED FAMILY IN MADISON WI

Boss:	Carlo Capieto
	Reign: 1970's
Underboss:	Joseph Aiello
	A different Joe Aiello than the one in the Unione Siciliano of Chicago
	Died: November 7, 1970

THE MINNEOPOLIS, MN

EARLY INDEPENDENT GROUP

MINNEAPOLIS, MN

INDEPENDENNT JEWISH GROUP – 1920's—1930's

SOME MEMBERS:	Yiddie Bloom
Harry Bloom
Israel "Ice Pick" Alderman
Isadore "Kid Cann" Blumenfield
Bernard Nemerov
Leon Gleckman
John Pullman

Minneapolis was represented at the 1929 Atlantic City Crime Convention.

THE CHICAGO, IL FAMILY

CHICAGO FAMILY

SOME CHICAGO GANGS AND MEMBERS

Regen's Colts – South Side – Formed 1902
Frank Regen, Mike Regen, Simon Gorman

Ralph Sheldon's Gang – Joined Capone's outfit in 1925

Vincent "The Schemer" Drucci Gang:
Born: 1895
Killed by police April 3, 1927
Louis "Two Gun" Alterie
Real Name: Leland Verain
Born: 1892, Colorado
Murdered: 1935
This gang joins the O'Bannion Gang in 1923

Valley Gang – West Side – Formed 1895 – 1920:
Terry Drugan, Died 1932
Frank Lake
This gang joins Johnny Torrio in 1920

Saltis – McErlane Gang – Southwest Side:
Joseph "Polock Joe" Saltis,
Frank McErlane, Died 1932
Vincent McErlane
John "Dingbat" Oberta
This gang joins Johnny Torrio by 1924

Maurice "Mossy" Enright Gang – Formed 1905

Murdered 1920 by The Black Handers for Big Tim Murphy

Big Tim Murphy Gang – Formed early 1900's:
Big Tim Murphy, Murdered 1928
John Powers

O'Donnell Gang – West Side – Formed 1907:
William "Klondike" O'Donnell
Brothers: Barnard O'Donnell
Miles O'Donnell, Murdered April 27, 1926
This gang joins Capone's outfit in 1927

O'Donnell Gang – South Side – Formed 1907:
An enemy gang to the Klondike O'Donnell's.
Edward "Spike" O'Donnell, Steve O'Donnell, Tom O'Donnell, Walter O'Donnell, Murdered 1925
This gang joins the Moran gang in 1927

Black Handers:
Salvatore "El Diavolo" Cardinella, Born 1880, Hung 1921
Nicholas Viana, Frank Campione, Vincenzo "Jim" "Sunny" Cosmano

Guilfoyle Gang – Northwest Side:
Martin Guilfoyle, Matthew Kolb, Al Winge
This gang joins the Torrio gang.

Circus Gang – Northwest Side:
John "Screwy" Moore Alias Claude Maddox
Anthony "Tony" Accardo
This gang joins Torrio's gang.

Forty Seconders Gang – Formed 1925:
Joe Colaro, Sam Giancana, Charles Nicoletti, Albert Frabotta, William Aloisio, Frank Caruso, Willie Daddano, Rocco Potenzo, Patzy Steffanelli, Vincent Inserro
This gang joins the Capone gang.

Twentieth Ward Gang – Jewish Group:
Hershel Miller, Max Miller, Max Eisen, Isadore "Nigger" Goldberg, Benjamin "Buddy" Jacobson, Samuel "The Greener" Jacobson, David Edelman, Samuel "Nails" Morton; Killed accidentally in 1921, Sam Bloom; Murdered By 1928 disbanded and the members fell into Capone's or the O'Bannion's outfits

O'Bannion Gang – North Side – Irish Group:
The top gang of this era

Boss— Charles "Dion" "Deanie" O'Bannion
Born: 1892
Reign: ?—1924
Murdered: November 10, 1924

Boss - Hymie Weiss
Real Name: Earl Wajciechowski
Born: 1898
Reign: 1924—1926
Murdered: October 11, 1926

Boss - Vincent "Schemer" Drucci
Born: 1895
The only Italian in a gang of Irish and Jewish
Reign: 1926—1927
Killed by police April 3, 1927

Boss— George "Bugs" Moran
Born: 1893
Reign: 1927—1938
Gang disbanded
Goes to prison 1946
Dies in prison 1957

St. Valentines Day Massacre, February 14, 1929 was an unsuccessful attempt by the Capone group to murder George Moran.

OTHER GANGS IN CHICAGO

O'Hara Gang, Bimbooms, Deadshots, Thistles, Lake St. Gang, Market Streeters and the Twelfth St. Gang

North Side of Chicago

Boss- Monte Tennes, North Side
Gambling and wire service
Reign: 1890—?
Retired: 1928

Boss- Ross Prio
Real Name: Rosario Fabricini
Born: 1900
Arrives from Sicily 1909
Starts to take over North Side in 1930
Died: 1972

Underboss- Eddie Vogel, Formerly from Cicero

SOUTH AND WEST SIDES OF CHICAGO

Boss- Michael Cassius "King Mike" McDonald
Born: 1840
Died: 1907

Aldermen- Michael "Hinky Dink" Kenna
Born: 1858
John J. "Bath House John" Coughlin
Born: 1860

ALDERMAN WARS – 1916 – 1928

Boss- Diamond Joe Esposito
Born: 1872
Reign: 1905—1928

Murdered: March 1928

Boss-	Vincenzo "Big Jim" Colosimo
	Born: 1871, Cosenza, Italy
	Arrives in U.S.A. 1881, New York
	Went to Chicago 1895
	Reign: 1910—1920
	Murdered: May 11, 1920
	2 Brothers
Underboss-	John Torrio, a nephew through marriage
Associate-	Mayor William Thompson
	Born: 1867, Elected to office: 1915

SOUTH AND WEST SIDES OF CHICAGO
CHICAGO FAMILY

Boss-	Giovanni Johnny "The Brain" Torrio
	Born: 1882
	Arrives in U.S.A. 1884, New York
	Goes to Chicago for the first time in 1909
	Goes to Chicago permanently in 1915
	Reign: 1920—1925
	In 1922 Torrio starts to move into Cicero
	Shot and recovered January 24, 1925
	Went to Italy in 1925 and returns to U.S.A. in 1929
	Dies in New York April 1957
Underboss-	Alfonso Capone
Associates-	Lawrence "Dago Lawrence" Mangano,
	Murdered 1944
	Mike "De Pike" Heitler,
	Murdered April 30, 1931
	Antonio "Tony Mops" Volpe
	Claude Maddox, Died 1958
	Real Name: John Ed "Screwy" Moore
	Martin Guilfoyle & Frank Pope

SOUTH AND WEST OF CHICAGO AND CICERO

Boss-	Alfonso "Big Al" "Scarface" Capone
	Born: January 17, 1899
	He calls his organization "The Outfit"
	Goes to Chicago 1919 from New York
	Reign: 1925—1932
	By 1928 all gangs joined either Capone or Moran Gangs
	Attends the Atlantic City, NJ National Crime Convention May 13—16, 1929.
	Is jailed in Philadelphia May 1929 to March 1930
	Imprisoned: May 4, 1932 to January 19, 1939
	Died: January 25, 1947
	Brothers: Vincenzo "James" Capone Alias Richard James Hart, Born1887; leaves home in NY at the age of 16 in 1904; becomes a Marshall in Homer, Nebraska; returns to his siblings in 1940's; Died 1952 Raffaele "Ralph" "Bottles" Capone; Born 1893; Died 1974 Salvatore Alias Frank Capone; Born 1895; Killed by police 1924
	Amadeo Alias John "Mimi"Capone, Umberto Alias Albert J. Capone, Matthew N. Capone; Died 1967
Underboss-	Frank "The Enforcer" Nitti
Consigliere-	Antonio "The Scouge" Lombardo
	Born: 1892
	Murdered: 1927
Consigliere-	Paul Ricca
Treasurer-	Jake "Greasy Thumb" Guzik
	Born: 1887, Moscow, Russia
	Died: February 21, 1956
Capos-	Calogero "Charles" Fischetti, Died 1951
	Rocco Fischetti
	Giuseppe "Joe" Fischetti, Fled to Brazil

St. Valentine's Day Massacre February 14, 1929 was an unsuccessful attempt by the Capone group to murder George "Bugs" Moran. The 7 men who were murdered are:

Fred Gusenberg
Pete Gusenberg – Born 1889
Al Weinshank
James Clark – Born 1887
John May – Born 1886 – Auto Mechanic
Adam Heyer – Born 1894 – Accountant
Dr. Reinhart Schwimmer – Optometrist

Thought to be triggermen on February 14, 1929 were:

Boris Chapman   Fred Burke
John Scalise   Albert Anselmi
Anthony Accardo   Frank Figenti
Machine Gun Jack McGurn

The only survivor was John May's german shepard dog named Hiball.

Assigned by President Calvin Coolidge and later reassigned by President Herbert Hoover to correct the problems in Chicago were Secretary of Treasury, Andrew Mellon, the IRS boss in Chicago Arthur P. Madden and FBI boss, J. Edgar Hoover in 1928. Head Attorney for this project was boss, George Johnson. Prosecuting Attorney for IRS in 1930 was Elmer Irey, Frank Wilson, Advisor Mike Malone, street boss was Eliot Ness.

Al Capone was charged with tax evasion. He claimed $150,000 and they proved that he made $215,000, therefore he was found guilty. Capone was sentenced to 10 years May 4, 1932 to may 3, 1942, released January 19, 1939.

The 9 Untouchable Members

Marty Lahart	Barny Cloonan
Paul Robsky	Mike King
Torn Fleir	Miles Chapman
Joe Leason	Bill Gardner
Sam Seager	

After a while two of them became touchable.

Associate in the Trans-National Wireless Service-
    Moses Annenberg
    Born: 1878
    Imprisoned: 1940
    Died: 1942
    Older brother Max Annenberg and Son Walter Annenberg

Associates- Joe Epstein, Harry Guzik, both Sam Bloom and Willie Bioff murdered

Bodyguards- Vincenzo "James" de Mora Alias Vincenzo Gibaldi, Alias "Machine Gun" Jack McGurn
    Born: 1904
    Murdered: February 13, 1936
    Frankie Rio; Real Name: Frank Kline

Bodyguards: Louis "Little New York" Campagna
    Born: 1900
    Died: 1955
    Filippo "PHIL" D'Andrea, Died 1950
    Sam "Golf Bag" Hunt; Real Name: Samuel McPherson
    Died: 1956

Acting Boss For Capone while he's in prison - Frank Nitti
    Real Name: Francesco Rafeale Nitto
    Born: 1884, Italy
    Shot and wounded 1932
    Reign: 1932-1938
    Goes to prison for 18 months 1933-1934

The Genealogy of American Organized Crime   [157]

	Leaves in charge Ralph Capone and Charles Fischetti Suicide: March 19, 1943
Underboss-	Anthony Accardo
Consigliere-	Paul Ricca, (who is really in control of this family at this time using Frank Nitti as a front)
Capos-	Frank Diamond Real Name: Frank Maritote Charles "Cherry Nose" Gioe Imprisoned: 1943—1947 Murdered: 1954

Associated With-Mayor William "Big Boy" Thompson
        Born: 1867
        Elected to office: 1915
        Died: March 19, 1944
        Lost election to Mayor Anton J. Cermak
        Cermak murdered 1933
        Gangster partner of Cermak is Teddy Newberry
        Murdered: 1932

Owner of the Continental Press Service (Wireless) -
        James M. Ragen
        Foe of the Capone Organization
        In business 1940 after Moe Annenberg had gone to prison
        Murdered: June 1946

CONTINUING CHICAGO FAMILY

Boss-	Paolino "Paul The Waiter" Ricca Real Name: Felice Delucia Born: 1897, Sicily Arrives in U.S.A. 1920 Reign: 1938—1956 Goes to prison 1943—1947 In 1959 was deported but never left the U.S.A. Died: 1972

	Underboss & Acting boss while Ricca is in prison-
Boss-	Antonino "Tony" "Joe Batters" "Big Tuna" Accardo
	Born: April 28, 1906
	Reigned together with Ricca 1947—1956
	Died: May 27, 1992
	Brother Martin
Underboss-	Charles Fischetti, Reign: 1938—1946
Underboss-	Sam Giancana, Reign: 1946 on
Consigliere & North Side Boss-	
	Ross Prio
	Real Name: Rosario Fabricini
	Born: 1900, Sicily
	Arrives in U.S.A. 1909
	Died: 1972
	His underboss Edward Vogel
Treasurers-	Jake Guzik,
	Murray "The Camel" "Mr. Fixit" "The Hump" Humphreys
	Real Name: Murray Llewellyn
	Born: 1899 in Wales
	Died: 1965
	Gus Alex
	Born: 1916 in Greece
	Joseph Glimco
Capo-	Gaspare Matrange— Calumet City, IL
Capo-	Anthony Musso, Died: May 22, 1958— Rockford, IL
Capo-	Anthony Pinelli, Born: 1899, Sicily— Gary, IN
Boss-	Salvatore "Sam" "Mooney" "MoMo" Giancana
	Born: June 15, 1908
	Reign: 1956—1965
	Murdered: June 19, 1975
	Brothers Chuck and Joseph

Underboss-	Sam "Teets" Battaglia
	Born: 1908
	Imprisoned: 1967
	Died in prison 1973
	Brother Paul Battaglia murdered
Consigliere-	Felix "Milwaukee Phil" Alerisio
	Born: 1908
	Imprisoned: 1967
	Died in prison 1971
Advisors & Elder Statesmen for Giancana-	
	Paul Ricca & Tony Accardo
Bodyguards-	Salvatore "Mad Dog Sam" DeStefano
	Born: 1909
	Murdered: 1973
	2 Brothers: Mario DeStefano & Michael DeStefano (who was murdered by his own brother Sam)
	Fiore "Fifi" Buccieri
	Born: 1905
	Died: 1973
	1 Brother Frank Buccieri
	David Yaras, Richard Cain
	Murdered December 20, 1973
	Charles "Chuckie" Nicoletti Murdered 1977,
	Guy Bannister Murdered,
	Willie "Potatoes" Daddano Imprisoned 1968,
	Leonardo "Needles" Gianola,
	Fat Leonard Caifano Murdered 1951,
	Marshall Caifano
Capo-	Frank Liparoto Alias La Porte- Calumet City, IL
Capo-	Gaspar Calo— Rockford, IL
Capo-	Joe Aiuppa— Cicero, IL
Capo-	Anthony Pinelli— Gary, IN

Capo-	Johnny Roselli— Las Vegas & Los Angeles, Murdered 1976, Associate to Roselli is Lewis McWillie
Consigliere-	Ross Prio
Boss-	Giuseppe "Joe" Aiuppa Born: December 1, 1907 Reign: 1965—1986
Underboss-	John Cerone
Consigliere-	Joseph Ferriola
Capo-	Frank Liparoto— Calumet City, IL
Capo-	Joseph Zammuto— Rockford, IL
Capo-	Dominic Brancato
Capo-	Marshall Caifano
Elder Statesman-	Tony Accardo
Boss-	John "Jackey The Lackey" Cerone Born: 1914 Reign: 1986—1987
Underboss-	Joseph Ferriola
Consigliere-	Joseph "The Clown" Lombardo
Capo-	Frank Buscemi— Rockford, IL
Boss-	Joseph Ferriola Born: ? Reign: 1987 – 1989 Died: 1989
Underboss-	Sam Anthony Carlisi (Also Acting Boss) Died: 1997
Consigliere-	Joseph Lombardo
Statesman-	Anthony Accardo
Boss-	John "No Nose" DiFronzo Reign: Late 1990's—?
Underboss-	?
Consigliere-	Angelo LaPietra
Advisor-	Joseph Lombardo

Capo Westside-
	Anthony Centraccio
Capo Southside-
	Joseph Monteleone
Capo Northside-
	Joseph Andriacchi

UNIONE SICILIANO EVENTUALLY NAME CHANGED TO ITALO-AMERICAN NATIONAL UNION

There were various chapters throughout the country and more than one in Chicago.

This is the Genealogy of Presidents of one of the Chicago chapters

President- Anthony D'Andrea
A lawyer and politician
Reign: ?—1921
Murdered: May 11, 1921
Brother Joseph, Murdered: 1913
Brother Filippo (bodyguard for Capone)
Brother Horace

President- Michele "Mike" Merlo
Reign: 1921—1924
Died: November 8, 1924 of natural causes

President- Angelo Genna
The Genna family arrives from Marsala, Sicily 1894
The family had been in the Bootlegging business since before Prohibition.
Reign: November 1924—1925
Murdered: May 26, 1925
Brothers: Salvatore "Sam" Genna, Born: 1884, Vincenzo "Jim" Genna, Peter Genna, Antonio "Tony" Genna, Murdered: July 8, 1925,

Mike Genna, Killed by police June 1925
Jim Genna returns to Sicily late 1920's
Other members of the Genna group:
Orazio Tropea, Vito Bascone, Filippo Gnolfo,
Tony Finalli and Giuseppe Nerone Alias
IL Cavaliere

PRESIDENCY VACANT FROM MAY 26, 1925 TO JULY 1925

President-   Samootso Amatuna
             Reign: July 1925—November 1925
             Murdered: November 1925

President-   Antonio "Tony" Lombardo
             Born: 1892
Consigliere for Capone—Appointed to this position by Capone
             Reign: November 1925—1927
             Murdered: September 7, 1927

President-   Pasquale Lolordo
             Reign: September 1927—1928
             Murdered: February 1928

President-   Joseph "Hop Toad" Giunta
             Reign: February 1928—1929
             Murdered: May 7, 1929
Vice-President- John Scalise, Murdered: May 7, 1929
Vice President- Albert Anselmi, Murdered: May 7, 1929
             All three murdered by Capone

President-   Joseph Aiello
             Born: 1891
Reigned while Capone was in prison in Philadelphia, PA
Foe of Al Capone
             Reign: May 1929—1930
             Murdered: October 23, 1930

9 Brothers altogether: Dominic Aiello, Murdered: 1927, Andrew Aiello, Antonio Aiello and 5 others

President-   Agostino Loverdo
             Reign: 1930—1931
             Murdered: 1931

President-   Filippo "Phil" D'Andrea
             Bodyguard to Capone
             Appointed by Capone
             Reign: 1931—?
             Died: 1950's

ANOTHER CHAPTER IN CHICAGO IN 1927

President-   Judge Bernard Barasa
Vice President- Constantino Vitello

THE NATIONAL UNIONE SICILIANO PRESIDENT OF
THE 1920'S
TILL HIS MURDER ON JULY 1, 1928
FRANKIE YALE OF BROOKLYN, NEW YORK

THE SPRINGFIELD, IL FAMILY

SPRINGFIELD & SOUTHERN ILLINOIS FAMILY

Little is ever publicly reported about this family.
An active, separate family from Chicago.
It is however a recognized family within the National Organized Crime Organization.

Boss: Frank Zito
            Reign: ?—1974
Was in attendance at the 1957 Apalachin Crime Convention
Died: August 22, 1974

Boss: ?
            Reign: 1974—?

THE KANSAS CITY, MO FAMILY

KANSAS CITY FAMILY

BLACKHANDERS
Peter DiGiovanni
Joseph "Scarface"DiGiovanni

INDEPENDENT
Soloman "Cutcher-Head-Off" "Solly" Weissman
Prominent around the 1920's

POLITICAL LEADER
Tom Pendergast
Reign: 1920's—late 1939
Imprisoned for 15 months
Successor: Jim Pendergast (Nephew)

Boss: John Lazia
             Reign: ?—1934
             Murdered: July 10, 1934

Boss: Charles Carollo
Reign: 1934—1939
Imprisoned: 1939
Deported: 1954
Underboss: James DeSimone
Underboss: Joseph DeLuca
Underboss: Nicolo Impostato

Boss: Vincenzo "Jim" Balestrere
                 Reign: 1939—1950
                 Murdered: 1950
Underboss: Charles Binaggio (Politics)
                 Born: 1909,
                 Murdered: April 6, 1950
Underboss: Charles Gargotta
                 Murdered: 1950
Underboss: Anthony Gizzo
Consigliere: Gaetano "Tano"Lococo
                 Imprisoned

Boss: Anthony Gizzo
                 Reign: 1950—1953
                 Died: April 1, 1953

Boss: Nicholas Civella
                 Born: 1912
                 Reign: 1953—1983
                 Imprisoned: 1980
                 Died in prison 1983
Underboss: Carlo DeLuno
Consigliere: Carlo Civella (Brother)
                 Died in Prison 1994

Duo acting bosses from 1980-1983 Carlo DeLuno and Carlo Civella

Boss: William Cammisano Sr.
                 Born: 1918
                 Reign: 1983—?
                 Died: 1995
Underboss: Peter J. Simmone

THE ST. LOUIS, MO FAMILY

ST. LOUIS FAMILY
Gangs around the Turn of the 20th Century

Egan's Rats Gang
(Primarily Irish and Jewish and a few young Italians)
Leader: William "Jellyroll" Egan
                Reign: 1900—1920's
                Murdered
Leader: Dinty Colbeck
                Reign: 1920's—1938
                Murdered

   Some other members of the Egan's Rats Gang:
   Thomas "Yonnie" Licavoli, Max "Big Maxey" Greenberg (Goes to Detroit), Earl Burke, Ray Burke, Fred Burke

Hogan Gang (Irish)
Cuckoos Gang (Syrian)
Green Dagoes Gang (Sicilians): Prominent around 1915
Some Members: Vito Giannola, John Giannola,
               Alphonso Palizzola,
               Amato Benedello (Murdered 1927)
Boss: Carmelo Fresina
               Reign: ? -1940
               Murdered: 1940

Boss: Antonio Lapiparo

	From Kansas City
	Reign: 1941—?
Underboss:	Tomaso Buffa
	Murdered: 1949
Associates:	Frank "Buster" Wortman
	Born: 1903, Died: 1970

Charles "Kewpie" Rich, Sidney Wyman, Jimmy Michaels, Morris Shenker

Boss:	John Vitale Sr.
	Reign: 1950's—1961
	Died: 1961

A PROMINENT SYRIAN MOB IN ST. LOUIS IS LED BY A MR. LEISURE

Boss:	Anthony Giordano
	Born: June 24, 1914
	Reign: 1960's—1970's
	Imprisoned: 1972
	Died: 1980
Underboss:	Anthony Sansone
Consigliere:	John Vitale Jr.
Advisors:	Sam Vitale of New Orleans
	Ralph Quasarano of Detroit
	Frank Coppola of Sicily
Associate:	James J. Carroll

Boss:	James Giammanco
	Reign: 1970's—1980's
Underboss:	Anthony Giacomo
Consigliere:	Anthony Vitale

Boss:	Matthew Trupiano
	Born: 1938
	Imprisoned: 1993—1995
	Reign: 1980's—?

                    Died: October 1997
Underboss: Joseph Camanata
Consigliere: Anthony Latino

THE TAMPA BAY, FL FAMILY

TAMPA BAY, FL FAMILY

Boss:	Ignacia Antinori
	Reign: ?—1930's
	Murdered: October 22, 1940
Underboss:	James Lumia
	Murdered: 1950
Associate:	Charles Wall (Gambling)
	Murdered: 1955
Boss:	Santo Trafficante Sr.
	Born: 1886
	Arrived in U.S.A. 1904
	Reign: Late 1930's—1954
	Died: 1954
Underboss:	Salvatore Scaglione
	Died
Underboss:	Gaetano Mistretta
Boss:	Santo Louis Trafficante Jr.
	Born: 1914
	5 Brothers: Samuel, Henry and 3 others
	Reign: 1954—1987
	Died: March 18, 1987
Underboss:	Frank Diecidue
	Imprisoned: 1976
Underboss:	Samuel Cacciatore

Consigliere: Gaetano Mistretta
Consigliere: Salvatore Scaglione

Boss: Joseph LoScalzo
Reign: 1990's—?
Underboss: Francesco DiCarla
Underboss: Alfonso Scaglione

MIAMI, FL

AN OPEN CITY

MIAMI, FL
AN OPEN CITY

Little Augie Pisano
Real Name: Antonino "Anthony" Carfano
Goes to Miami from New York City 1933
Is backed by Joe Adonis
Steps down for Lansky in the 1940's
Murdered in New York City September 29. 1959

Meyer Lansky
Declares Miami an open city
Arrives permanently in Miami 1953
Associates in Miami:
Jake Lansky   Sam Cohen
Harold Salvey   Charles Friedman
Herman Stark   Ed Rosenbaum
Frank Erickson   John Pullman
Ron Sacco
Vincenzo "Jimmy Blue Eyes" Alo
Benjamin Kramer (Protégé of Lansky)
Robert S. Vesco was affiliated in the late 1960's
Howard Garfinkle affiliated in the mid 1970's in New Jersey

THE NEW ORLEANS, LA FAMILY

NEW ORLEANS FAMILY

SOME GANGS

YELLOW HENRY GANG

LIVE OAKS GANG

Boss-	Giuseppe Esposito Reign: 1880—1890's Deported Foe: Anthony Labruzzo, Murdered 1881
Boss-	Giuseppe Macheca Born: Sicily Reign: 1888—1890 Killed with 10 others on March 16, 1890 for the murder of Police Chief David Hennessey. Others killed by vigilantes: Antonio Scarffidi, Antonio Bagnetto, Manuel Polutz, Peter Natali, Antonino Marchessi, Charles Traina, Petro Marnastino, Salvatore Sincesi, Donito Comitz, Bastian Incardona
Associate-	Antonio Matranga

A 2ND Fraction during this period is the **PROVENZANO BROTHERS GROUP** many of which were murdered by the Matranga group.

Boss-   Antonio Matranga
                  Reign: 1891—?
                  Pass leadership to his brother

Black Hander-   Paolo Marchese,
                  Prominent around 1910

Boss-   Carlo "Charlie" Matranga
                  Born: 1857, Palermo, Sicily
                  Reign: ?—1922
                  Retired: 1922
                  Died: October 28, 1943
Associates-   Sam Carolla, Nicholo Favia

Boss-   Sylvestro "Sam" Carolla
                  Born: 1896
                  Arrived in U.S.A. 1904
                  Reign: 1922—1947
                  Deported 1947, Returned 1949
                  Deported again 1950, Returned 1970 to U.S.A.
                  Died: 1972
Underboss-   Corrado Giacona
                  Died: July 25, 1944
                  Members of his immediate family eventually
                  moved to Detroit
Underboss-   Frank Todaro
                      Died: November 29, 1944
                      Members of his immediate family eventually
                      moved to Buffalo, NY
Underboss-   Nicholas Marcello
                  Cousin to Carlos Marcello
Consigliere-   Charlie Matranga
Consigliere-   Nofio Pecora
Capos-   Tomaso Rizzuto, Giuseppe Capro, Francesco
                  Lombardino, Nicholas Grifazzi

Associated with:	Governor Huey "Kingfish" Long
	Born: 1893
	Murdered: September 10, 1935
	Frank Costello of New York, goes to New Orleans in 1934 to operate slot machine business and gambling
	Costello leaves in charge Phillip "Dandy Phil" Kastel
	Born: 1886; Suicide: August 16, 1962
	Also Costello's brother-in-law Dudley Geigerman And Seymour Weiss
Boss-	Carlos Marcello
	Real Name: Calogero Minicari
	Born: February 6, 1910, Tunisia Africa of Sicilian Parents
	Arrives in U.S.A. 1911
	Reign: 1947—Mid 1990's
	Deported to Guatemala in the 1950's and returned on his own.
	Died: 1993
	Brothers Joe, Pete (Born: 1921), Sam, Pat (Born: 1925), Tony and Vince
Underboss-	Mario Marino
Underboss-	Joseph Marcello
Consigliere-	Peter Marcello
Advisor-	G. Wray Gill
Capo-	Frank Caracci in the 1980's
Boss-	Anthony Carolla
	Reign: 1993—?

THE DALLAS, TX FAMILY

DALLAS, TX FAMILY

Boss-   Carlo Piranio
                   Born: ?
                   Reign: ?—1928
                   Died: February 20, 1930

Boss-   Joseph Piranio
                   Born: ?
                   Brother of Carlo
                   Reign: 1928—1946
                   Suicide: October 27, 1956
Associate-   Lester "Benny" Binion
                   Eventually goes to Las Vegas

           ARRIVALS FROM CHICAGO IN 1946:
   Pasquale Manno, Dan Lardino, Jack Nappi, Paul Labriola and Paul Jones
             ARRIVAL FROM NEW ORLEANS:
   Sam Maceo, Died: April 16, 1951

Boss-   Joseph Civello
                   Born: 1902
                   Went to prison in 1964
                   Reign: 1946—1964
                   Died: January 17, 1970

THE DALLAS FAMILY AS A SEPARATE FAMILY DISBANDS AT THIS TIME.

DALLAS NOW A BRANCH AFFILIATE OF THE NEW ORLEANS FAMILY.

Boss-   Joseph Campisi
              Born: ?
              Reign: 1964—?
Underboss-   Sam Campisi (Brother of Joseph Campisi)
              Died: 1970
              Campisi family members arrested in mid 1990's
Associate-   Frank Fiorini Alias Frank Sturgis

THE DENVER, CO FAMILY

DENVER, CO FAMILY

Boss- Pelligrino Scaglia
Reign: ?—1922
Murdered: May 5, 1922

Boss- Giuseppe Roma
Reign: 1922—1933
Murdered: 1933

Boss- Calogero Blanda
Reign: 1933—1946

Boss- James Coletti
Reign: 1946—1969
Died: July 28, 1975

Underboss- Anthony Biase
Born: 1908

Boss- Joseph Spinuzzi
Affiliated with New Orleans Family
Reign: 1969—1975
Died: September 6, 1975

Boss- Eugene Smaldone
Born: 1910
Reign: 1975—1983
Imprisoned: 1983

	Died: 1992
Underboss-	Clarence Smaldone (brother)
	Imprisoned: 1983
	Another brother Clyde Smaldone
Consigliere-	Paul Villano
	Imprisoned: 1983

LAS VEGAS, NV

AN OPEN CITY

LAS VEGAS, NV
OPEN CITY FOR ALL FAMILIES

From California pre Bugsy Siegel
Antonio Strolla
Alias Tony Cornero
Born: 1900
Died: 1955

Benjamin Bugsy Siegel - opens Flamingo Casino Hotel on December 26, 1946 in behalf of Meyer Lansky, Charlie Luciano, Frank Costello, Joe Adonis and other organized crime investors.
Host of opening night is actor George Raft.
Entertainer – Jimmy Durante
Band Leader – Xavier Cugot
Bugsy Siegel murdered in Los Angeles June 20, 1947
His girlfriend, Virginia Hill; Born: 1918, Suicide: 1966

Moe Dalitz
In behalf of the Cleveland Syndicate and the Cleveland Family,……..The Desert Inn.

Meyer Lansky and Associates:

Ben Seigelbaum, Alvin I. Malnik, John Pullman, Moe Rosen, Ed Levinson, Allen R. Glick, Alan Cohen, Joel Cohen, Sidney Korshak, Irving Devine, Moe Sedway, Abe Pritzker, Stanford Clinton, Arthur Greene, Paul Dorfman, Allen Dorfman (Murdered 1982), Ed Cellini, Dino Cellini, Gus Greenbaum (Murdered October 1958) and Vincenzo "Jimmy Blue Eyes" Alo

Johnny Roselli
In behalf of the Chicago outfit
Real Name: Fillipo Sacco
Born: 1905, Esteria, Italy
Murdered: 1976
Operation Mongoose of 1960 involved the C.I.A.'s plot through Jimmy Hoffa (murdered 1975) with organized crime to murder Fidel Castro. Organized crime members involved were Johnny Roselli and Sam Giancano from the Chicago Family, Tony Provenzano from the NJ branch of the Genovese Family, Salvatore Grunello and James Plumeri from the Lucchese Family, Russell Buffalino from the Pittston, PA Family, John Larocca and Gabriel Mannarino of the Pittsburgh, PA Family, Tony Giacolone of the Detroit Family, and Santo Trafficante Jr. of the Tampa Bay Family.

Chicago Family Representative in Las Vegas
Anthony Spilotro Born: 1938 Went to Vegas in 1971
Murdered: 1986

THESE FAMILIES ARE THOUGHT TO HAVE HIDDEN INTERESTS IN THESE CASINOS
During the 1950's, 60's, and 70's

DESERT INN	Moe Dalitz—Cleveland, OH
SANDS HOTEL	Meyer Lansky, Edward Levinson, Joe "Doc" Stacher—New York & Chicago

HORSESHOE CLUB	Lester "Benny" Binion, Sam Mateo Dallas and Los Angeles
FLAMINGO HOTEL	Benjamin "Bugsy" Siegel, Gus Greenbaum, Meyer Lansky, Charlie Luciano, Frank Costello, Joe Adonis—New York & others
TROPICANA HOTEL	Frank Costello—New York, Phillip "Dandy Phil" Kastel—New Orleans, Joe Agosto—Kansas City
DUNES HOTEL	Raymond Patriarca—New England, Matthew Ianniello—New York & Morris Shenker
FRONTIER HOTEL	Detroit & St. Louis
SAHARA HOTEL	Meyer Lansky, Jake Lansky
STARDUST HOTEL	Frank Rosenthal, Allen Glick Chicago, Los Angeles, Kansas City, Cleveland and Milwaukee
RIVIERA HOTEL	Meyer Lansky, Charles Luciano New York
SILVER SLIPPER	Irving "Niggy" Devine, Meyer Lansky
FREMONT CASINO	Irving "Niggy" "Devine, Meyer Lansky
THUNDERBIRD	Meyer Lansky, Willie Cohen
ALADDIN HOTEL	Sorkis Webbe—Detroit & St. Louis
CAESARS PALACE	Jay Scarno—Chicago, New York, New England
CIRCUS CIRCUS	Allen Glick & Argent Corp.

MR. LAS VEGAS PARRY THOMAS

THE LOS ANGELES, CA FAMILY

LOS ANGELES, CA FAMILY

EARLY YEARS
FRACTION I

Giuseppe "Joseph" Ardizzone
Reign: 1920's
Murdered: October 15, 1931
Vincenzo Zorra Alias Jimmy Schafer Alias James Fagarty

FRACTION II
Domenico "Danto" D'Crolla
Emilio Georgettie, Died
Sam Mateo goes to Las Vegas in 1947, Take over of Lester "Benny" Binion's interests at that time.

L.A. FAMILY RECOGNIZED BY NATIONAL SYNDICATE IN 1937

Boss-   Jack Dragna
              Real Name: Anthony Rizzoti
              Born: 1891
              Arrives in U.S.A. 1914 from Corleone, Sicily
              Reign: 1931—1957
              Died: February 23, 1957
Underboss-   Guglielmo "Momo" Adamo

	Suicide: 1957
Consigliere-	Thomas Dragna (Brother)
Associate-	Harold Meltzer
Associate-	Arthur Samish (Politics) Between 1939—1956

Benjamin Bugsy Siegel
Goes to Los Angeles 1937
Takes over some of Jack Dragna's gambling interests
Opens Flamingo Casino Hotel in Las Vegas December 26, 1946
Sent ahead to Las Vegas Morris Sidwirz Alias Moe Sedway
Also Phillip "Little Farvel" "The Stick" Kovolick,
Murdered September 16, 1949
And Hymen "Curley" Holtz

An Independent Bookmaker in Los Angeles at the time of Siegel's arrival in Los Angeles. Became an associate of Siegel in Los Angeles

Mickey Cohen
Born: 1913
Formerly of the Cleveland Syndicate
5 attempts by the Dragna Family of murder on his life, all failed
Imprisoned: 1952—1956 and again 1962—1972
Died: 1976

Boss-	Frank DiSimone
	An attorney
	Reign: 1957—1968
	Died: 1968
Underboss-	Simone Scozzari
	Deported: 1962
Underboss-	Nick Licato
	Formerly of Detroit
Capo-	Anthony Marcello
	Formerly of New Orleans
Associate-	In Las Vegas Louis "Scarface" Lieberman

Alias Lou Green

Boss- Nick Licate
Born: 1897 in Camporeale, Sicily
Arrives in U.S.A. 1913
Reign: 1968—1974
Removed from the Detroit Family
Imprisoned: 1969—1970
Died: 1974
Underboss- Joseph Dippolito
Consigliere- Thomas Palermo

Boss- Dominic Brooklier
Real Name: Dominic Brucceleri
Alias Jimmy Regace
Born: 1914
Reign: 1974—1984
Died in prison: July 1984
Underboss- Sammy Sciortino
Consigliere- Thomas Palermo
Capo- Frank Buccieri
Associate- Allen Glick

While Brooklier is imprisoned for a short stay around 1980 Dual Acting Bosses Aladena "Jimmy The Weasel" Fratianno Born 1913 and Louis T. Dragna

Boss- Louis Thomas Dragna
Nephew of Jack Dragna and son of Thomas Dragna
Born: July 18, 1920
Reign: 1984—1986
Underboss- Mike Rizzitello
Consigliere- Sam Sciortino
Consigliere- Jack LoCicero

Boss- Peter Milano (Son of the Milano's of Cleveland)
Born: 1925
Reign: 1986—?
Underboss- Carmen Milano (brother)

Consigliere-   Jack LoCicero

SAN DIEGO-A BRANCH AFFILIATE OF THE LOS ANGELES FAMILY

Boss-   Frank "Bomp" Bompensiero
Reign: 1945—1955
Imprisoned: 1955
Released: ?
Consigliere for the Los Angeles Family 1976—1977
Murdered: February 10, 1977

Boss-   Antonio Mirabile
Born: Alcoma, Sicily
Reign: 1955—1958
Murdered: December 27, 1958

Boss-   Joseph Adamo
Brother Guglielmo "Momo" Adamo
Reign: 1959—?

2ND FRACTION

Matranga Family of Detroit at this time starts to move into San Diego

Brothers: Frank, Leo & Joseph Matranga
Reign: 1959—1968

Chris Petti from Chicago
Born: 1942 came later

THE SAN JOSE, CA FAMILY

SAN JOSE, CA FAMILY

Little is ever publicly reported about this family.

Boss-	Onofrio Sciortino
	Reign: ?—1959
	Died: September 10, 1959
Boss-	Joseph Cerrito
	Reign: 1959—Late 1980's
	Died: Late 1980's
Underboss-	?
Consigliere-	Stefano Zoccoli
Capo-	Angelo Marino

Some time after the death of Joseph Cerrito this family merges with the San Francisco, CA Family.

THE SAN FRANCISCO, CA FAMILY

SAN FRANCISCO, CA FAMILY

Little is ever publicly reported about this family.

Boss-   Francesco Lanza
                Reign: ?—1937
                Died: June 14, 1937

2nd FRACTION
Frank Scappatura
Others in the group:
John Franzone, Leonardo Calamia, James Lasala, Sabastiano Nami

Boss-   Anthony Lima Sr.
                Reign: 1937—1953
                Imprisoned: 1953
Underboss-   Gaspare "Bill"Sciortino
                Nick DeJohn from Chicago
                Murdered: May 9, 1947

Boss-   Michele Abati
                Reign: 1953—1961
                Deported: July 7, 1961
                Died: September 5, 1962

Boss-	James "Jimmy" Lanza
	Reign: 1961—1974
	Son of Francesco Lanza
	Died: 1974
Underboss-	Lou Lurie
Consigliere-	Gaspare "Bill" Sciortino
Boss-	Anthony Lima Jr.
	Reign: 1974—?
Underboss-	?
Consigliere-	?

In the late 1980's this family merges with the San Jose, CA Family.

CANADIAN FAMILY

AN INDEPENDENT GROUP

MONTREAL, CANADA INDEPENDENT OF THE U.S.A. FAMILIES DURING PROHIBITION

Legitimate Businessmen in Canada
Both sold booze to U.S.A. Bootleggers during Prohibition
Sam Bronfman: Born: 1891; Died: 1971
Of what is known as Seagrams Corporation

Lewis Rosentiel: Of what is known as Schenley Corporation

COTRONI FAMILY

A group that cooperates with all U.S.A. families
Boss- Vincent "Vic" Cotroni
Brothers: Frank Cotroni and Joe Cotroni
Reign: ?—1980's
Members- The Volpe Brothers
Paul Volpe, Albert Volpe and Eugene Volpe
Associate- John Pullman associated with Meyer Lansky
Born: 1903

SICILY FAMILIES

SICILY AND VARIOUS SMALL TOWNS AND THEIR BOSSES

Boss- Vito Cascio-Ferro
Born: 1862
Headquarters Palermo, Sicily
Capo Di Tutti Capri
Went to New York in 1900
Goes to New Orleans in 1902
Eventually goes back to Palermo
Murderer of New York Police Officer Giovanni Petrosino in Sicily in 1909
Reign: 1895—1929
Imprisoned: 1929
Died in Prison 1932
Underboss- Paolo Varsalona
Associate- Nicolo Gentile
Born: 1884
Goes to U.S.A., Joins Charlie Luciano. Returns to Sicily. Returns to U.S.A. and becomes Consigliere of the Pittsburgh Family
Associate- Salvatore Maranzano
Goes to New York in 1918
Returns to Sicily and goes back to New York in 1925 & 1927
Associate- Giuseppe Profaci
Goes to U.S.A. in 1922 and stays

Boss- Calogero Vizzini
Born: 1877 Villalba, Sicily

                        Joins Honor Society 1902
                        Becomes Capo Di Tutti Capri
                        Reign: 1929—1954
                        Died: 1954
Underboss-   Giuseppe Genco Russo
                        Murdered: 1950's

FROM LATE 1940'S TO MID 1980'S
SOME OTHER SMALL FAMILY BOSSES IN SICILY
Vanni Sacco, Antonio Cottone, Murdered: 1949
Angelo La Barbera   Salvatore La Barbera
Gaetano Filipone   Francesco Riccobono
Michele Navarra
Cesara "U Patra Nostra" Manzella, Murdered: 1963
Michele Sindona -Financier for the Sicilian Crime
Organization and the Vatican
Reign: 1940's—1980's
Imprisoned: 1980
Poisoned to death 1986 while in prison

FAMILY OF CINISI, SICILY
Boss-   Gaetano Badalamenti
                Born: 1923
                Reign: ?—1978 in Sicily
                Ousted by the Sicilian Commission
                Fled to South America

Replaced by the Sicilian Commission
Boss-   Antonio Badalamenti
                Cousin to Gaetano Badalamenti
                Reign: 1978—1981
                Murdered: 1981

FAMILY OF PALERMO, SICILY & HEAD OF COMMISSION
Boss-   Michele Grecco

	Reign: ?—1986
	Imprisoned: 1986
Underboss-	Filippo Guarino
Boss-	Antonino Geraci
	Born: 1929
	Reign: 1986—early 1990's
	Imprisoned and released in early 1997
	Murdered: November 23, 1997
Associate-	Piero Aglieri
	Born: 1959

OTHER SMALL TOWN BOSSES

Boss-	Licio Gelli
	Went to South America 1982
Boss-	Salvatore Inzerillo
	Murdered: 1981

PARTINICO SICILY FAMILY

Boss-	?
Underboss-	Filippo Nania

NOCE FAMILY OF CENTRAL PALERMO

Soldier in New York
Gaetano Mazzara
Murdered: 1986

SAN MARIA DI GESU FAMILY
Boss-	Stefano Bontade
	Reign: 1970's—1981
	Murdered: 1981

CIACULLI FAMILY
Boss-   Giuseppe "Pino" Greco
             Reign: Late 1970's to early 1980's

BAGBERIA FAMILY
Boss-   Leonardo Greco
             Reign: Mid 1970's to mid 1980's
Brother Salvatore Greco in New Jersey arrested in 1984

SAN GIUSEPPE IATO FAMILY
Boss-   Antonio Salamone
             Reign: Around 1980
             Goes to Brazil
Brothers Salvatore Salamone of Pennsylvania & Filippo Salamone of New Jersey
Associate-   Giuseppe Ganci of New York

CORLEONE FAMILY
Boss-   Luciano Liggio
             Born: 1960
             Reign: ?—1982
             Imprisoned: 1982
Underboss-   Simone Zito
Associates- New York Representative Rosario Nimo, Francesco "Cheech" Gambino, Imprisoned
New Jersey Dominic Manino, Imprisoned: 1988
Chicago Representative Carmine Esposito, Deported

CORLEONE FAMILY
Boss-   Salvatore "Toto" Riina
             Head of Commission
             Capo Di Tutti Capri
             Reign: 1982—1993
             Captured January 1993 received 9 life sentences
Underboss-   Bernardo Provenzano
             Born: 1934
Capo-   Leoluca Bagarella

Arrested: June 24, 1995

CORLEONE FAMILY
Boss-   Bernardo Provenzano
             Born: 1934
             Head of Commission
             Reign: 1993—?
Underboss-   LeoLuca Bagarella
             Brother-in-law of Salvatore Riina
             Arrested June 1995
Underboss-   Giovanni Brusca
             Born: 1958

PORTA NUOVA FAMILY
Boss-   Giuseppe "Pippo" Calo
             Reign: Late 1970's—1986
             Convicted
Associate-   Tomaso Buscetta
             Born: 1928
             Left Sicily for Argentina
             Went to Brazil 1951
             Went back to Sicily
             Imprisoned: 1972—1980
             Left again for Brazil 1983
             Imprisoned: 1984
Turned States Evidence, Enters Witness Protection Program

ANOTHER SMALL TOWN FAMILY IN SICILY
Boss-   Giuseppe Bono
             Reign: 1970's—1980's Sicily & Milano, Italy
             Arrives in New York 1980
             Lives in Pelham, New York
             Brother Alfredo Bono of Milan, Italy

BORGETTO FAMILY, SICILY

Boss-   ?
Associate-   Giuseppe Soresi
Cousin Salvatore Lamberti of Stone Ridge, New York
Cousin Giuseppe Lamberti of Menlo Park, New Jersey

CAMORRA OF NAPLES, ITALY

Boss-   Michele Zara
               Reign: Late 1970's to early 1980's
Affiliated with the Los Angeles Family in U.S.A.

Big trial of mafia members in Sicily on May 9, 1993. A combination courthouse and prison was built for this occasion. 467 men accused 344 were convicted

PIZZA CONNECTION OF NARCOTICS 1979—1987

PIZZA CONNECTION 1979—1987 OF NARCOTICS

Boss-   Gaetano Badalamenti of Rio De Janeiro, Brazil
           Convicted
Sons: Vito Badalamenti & Leonardo Badalamenti of Brazil

Salvatore "Toto" Catalano
Born: 1941 in Ciminna, Sicily
Arrives in U.S.A. 1966
Lives in Queens, New York
Becomes an Underboss in the Bonanno Family
Brothers: Vito & Dominic Catalano

Giuseppe Genci
Arrives in U.S.A. 1966 from San Giuseppe Iato, Sicily
Lived in Queens, New York
Died: February 1986 while on trial

ALL ARRESTED IN APRIL 1984, TRIAL STARTED SEPTEMBER 1985, CONVICTED APRIL 1987

CONTINUATION OF THOSE ARRESTED IN THE PIZZA CONNECTION

Pietro Alfano
Born: 1937

Arrives in U.S.A. 1963
Nephew of Gaetano Badalamenti
Lives in Oregon, IL
Shot and paralyzed for life February 1987 during trial
Convicted

Emanuele Palazzolo
Brother-in-law to Pietro Alfano
Lives in Milton, WI
Convicted

Samuel Evola
Nephew thru marriage to Gaetano Badalamenti
Lives in Temperance, MI
Convicted

Andrea Aiello
Lives in Buffalo, New York

Vincenzo Randazzo
Nephew of Gaetano Badalamenti
Lives in New York, Switzerland & Sicily
Deported

Salvatore Salamone
Brother of Antonio Salamone of Sicily & Filippo Salamone of NJ Lives in Bloomburg, PA
Convicted

Filippo Salamone
Lives in New Jersey
Convicted

Salvatore Lamberti
Cousin of Giuseppe Lamberti of New Jersey
Lives in Stone Ridge, New York
Both of the Borgetto Family, Sicily
Convicted

Giuseppe Lamberti
Lives in Menlo Park, New Jersey
Convicted

Salvatore Mazzurco
Brother-in-law of Giuseppe Lamberti
Lives in Baldwin, Long Island
Convicted

Giuseppe Soresi
of the Borgetto Family, Sicily
Convicted

Salvatore Greco
Brother of Leonardo Greco of Bagheria, Sicily
Lives in Oakhurst, New Jersey
Convicted

Giuseppe Bono
Lives in Pelham, New York, Milano, Italy & Sicily
Convicted

Francesco "Ciccio" Polizzi
Lives in Belleville, New Jersey
Member of the DeCalvacante Family
Convicted

Paolo LaPorta
Lives in Philadelphia, PA

Giovanni LaPorta
Lives in Philadelphia, PA

Alberto Ficalora
Lives in Philadelphia, PA

Gaetano Mazzara
Lives in Sayerville, New Jersey
Murdered during the trial November 1986

Frank Castronovo
Lives in Sayreville, New Jersey
Convicted

Cesara Bonventre
Lives in Brooklyn, New York
Murdered: 1984

Baldassare "Baldo" Amato
Lives in Brooklyn, New York
Convicted

Filippo Casamento
Lives in Brooklyn, New York
Convicted

Vito Badalamenti
Son of Gaetano Badalamenti
Acquitted

SUICIDES

SUICIDES

Frank Nitti   Chicago Family, 1943

Joseph Patirano   Dallas Family, 1956

Guglielmo "Momo" Adamo   Los Angeles Family, 1957

Abner "Longie" Zwillman   New Jersey, 1959

Phillip "Dandy Phil" Kastel   New Orleans, 1962

Virginia Hill Bag Woman for the Luciano Family, 1966

Louis Rothkopf, Alias Lou Rhody   Cleveland Syndicate

George Weingartner   New Jersey branch of the Genovese Family, July 5, 1998

Made in the USA
San Bernardino, CA
17 May 2014